THE ENERGY DIMENSION

THE ENERGY DIMENSION

*A practical guide to energy
in rural development programmes*

CHRISTOPHER HURST and ANDREW BARNETT
with contributions from *Michel Lagoutte,
Dr Jas Gill*, and *Dr Hamed Sow*

INTERMEDIATE TECHNOLOGY PUBLICATIONS 1990

Intermediate Technology Publications Ltd
103–105 Southampton Row, London WC1B 4HH, UK

ISBN 1 85339 074 7

A CIP catalogue record for this book is available from the British Library

Ce document est également publié en français — est disponible à:
Sussex Research Associates Ltd
33 Southdown Avenue, Brighton BN1 6EH, UK

Typeset by Inforum Typesetting, Portsmouth
and printed in Great Britain by Short Run Press, Exeter

Contents

Preface   ix
How to use this book   x

1 RECOGNIZING THE ENERGY DIMENSION   **1**

Energy and rural development   1
The key issues   4
  The dominance of woodfuels   4
  Petroleum products   7
  Rural electrification   7
  New and renewable energy technologies   8
Energy project planning   10

2 THE ADMINISTRATIVE OPTIONS   **13**

Action at the institutional level   14
  Responsibility   14
  Capability for energy planning   15
  Awareness of the energy dimension   16
  Procedures and standard terms of reference   17
  Inclusion of energy issues in project documentation   18
Action at the level of macro policy   19
The energy dimension at the level of projects and
  programmes   20
  Seven key factors for project success   21

3 ENERGY IN THE CONTEXT OF RURAL DEVELOPMENT   **24**

The rural sector and the dynamics of development   24
  Agricultural policies   25
  Rural financial institutions   28
  The evolution of development strategies   31
Traditional energy and rural development   36
  The woodfuel problem   36
  The use of woody biomass in households   38
  Wood, women and health   42

v

Competing demands for wood   44
Policy interventions for woodfuel   49
The necessity of an energy transition   56
Kerosene as a household fuel   57
Energy for agricultural mechanization   60
Energy for rural industries   67
Energy for rural transport   72
Energy for social projects   73
Conventional energy supplies   76
Renewable energy technologies   80

ANNEXE I: CHECK-LISTS   **90**

General check-list   90
Option matrix   95
Check-lists for specific types of project   96
Agricultural development   96
Farming systems and mechanization   96
Livestock   97
Fishery   98
Irrigation   98
Rural industries   99
Women's projects   100
Village water supply and sanitation   101
Rural health   101
Tourism   102
Telecommunications   103
Desertification and deforestation control   103
Resettlement and food aid   104
Transportation   104
Education   105

ANNEXE II: FACT SHEETS FOR RURAL ENERGY
SUPPLY OPTIONS   **106**

Contacts and references   106

Rural electrification   108
Grid extension   108
Autonomous production of electricity   109
Rural pre-electrification   110
Water-pumping systems   112
Classification   112
Village water supply systems   113

Autonomous pumping systems   113
   Handpumps and footpumps   114
   Animal-powered pumps   116
   Windmills   117
   Photovoltaic pumps   119

Energy conversion with renewable energy technologies   121

   Biomass conversion   121
   Densification   121
   Charcoal production   124
   Boilers   126
   Gasifiers   128
   Biogas   130
   Hydro plants   132
   Photovoltaic generators   134
   Solar water heaters   137
   Solar driers   138
   Aerogenerators   140

Energy conservation   143

Improved woodfuel stoves   143
Improved charcoal stoves   144
Internal combustion engines   145
Appliances for photovoltaic generators   147

ANNEXE III: BIBLIOGRAPHY   149

ANNEXE IV: EXPERTS WHO REVIEWED EARLIER DRAFTS   166

Preface

Energy should become one of the many automatic concerns for people involved with rural development in the Third World. The objective of this book is to show why energy is so important to rural development and to provide practical advice on incorporating the energy dimension into project planning.

Our focus is the energy dimension of those attempts to provide international aid to rural areas of developing countries which are not conventionally considered to be energy projects.

Our audience includes administrators, rural specialists, and activists in both donor and recipient countries who identify, design and implement rural schemes but who are not energy specialists. This primarily concerns the European Community and the associated African, Caribbean and Pacific States (the ACP), but the advice will also be relevant to the wider aid community.

It clearly is not possible to provide a guide that would allow readers to choose the correct technology for every energy end-use in all rural areas of all developing countries. However, the aim is to provide sufficient information to make it possible to pose the right questions to energy experts and the proposers of projects.

The book is based on the European Community's experience of energy aid over 25 years* and has benefited from the advice not only of the staff of the Commission but also of energy experts both in Europe and in developing countries (see Annexe IV for a full list of names).

Dr Hamed Sow contributed to the early stages of the work; Dr Jas Gill provided inputs to the check-lists; and Michel Lagoutte also worked on the Annexes and contributed a 'Francophone' perspective. Research assistance was provided by Bintou Sow, Dr Leslie Brattle and Elizabeth Marsh. However, the main authors alone are responsible for advice offered and for any errors and omissions that remain.

---

* See *An Evaluation of Energy Projects in ACP Countries*, A Synthesis Report to the European Commission and the Euorpean Investment Bank by Andrew Barnett and Julian Bharier of Sussex Research Associates Limited and Marita Konstancczak-Reyes and Klaus Bauman of Lahmeyer International GmbH (EEC DG VIII/EV, Brussels, May 1988, 115 pages plus annexes).

How to use this book

Aid administrators and people working in rural development typically have little time to read. The book is therefore written with this fact of life very much in mind.

Chapter 1 provides a brief summary of the most important elements of the energy dimension. Chapter 2 provides a brief guide to the options for administrative action. Chapter 3 provides more detailed explanation of energy in the context of rural development and provides an initial justification for the perspectives and recommendations of the book.

Detailed supplementary information is provided in the Annexes. Annexe I contains check-lists for each type of rural project. Annexe II contains rural energy supply option fact sheets.

Busy readers can limit themselves to reading just the headings and italic *key points* in Chapter 1 and 2. Each key point is expanded and explained in a few subsequent brief paragraphs. Those readers requiring more detail or more explanation can turn to the specific sub-section of Chapter 3, then to the Annexes and finally to additional sources of information listed in the Bibliography.

1 Recognizing the energy dimension

Energy and rural development

Why should we be concerned about energy in rural development?

Even when the energy crisis is not in the daily news, in rural areas energy problems are far from over.

○ In many regions the availability of woodfuel is decreasing rapidly as deforestation destroys the rural environment. More and more time has to be spent collecting fuel; inferior smoky fuels must be burnt; and adverse changes in diet are made.

○ Increases in agricultural productivity and rural incomes are often linked to the use of modern forms of energy. In India every 1 per cent growth in agricultural output is associated with a 3.5 per cent growth in the use of modern fuels. However, the modern fuels that can increase the productivity of rural labour, land, and capital are often just not available.

○ When the international price of oil measured in ECU is low, debt repayments and shortages of foreign exchange still make it expensive for many countries.

○ Even though national energy consumption is growing, the gap between consumption in urban areas and that in rural areas grows ever wider.

○ The uncontrolled removal of biomass for fuel exacerbates problems of erosion and flooding, and leads to the reduction in viability of other efforts at rural development.

○ Rural people find that fuel to cook their food becomes harder and harder to obtain. The time spent gathering fuel and cooking cannot be put to more productive or rewarding activities.

A common reaction of administrators[1] to this question has been that they are already working under great pressure, that rural development is a

---

[1] By the term 'administrator', we mean those persons in donor agencies and in recipient countries who design and implement rural development projects.

difficult business, and that energy has not been a significant input to rural development projects[2] in the past — so why add yet another burden to an already overburdened system?

Five administrative reasons for giving additional attention to energy in rural development

○ *The history of project failure* The 1970s and 1980s provided graphic illustrations of what happens to rural projects when oil products are not available or are prohibitively expensive; or when fuelwood shortage increases hardship, and diverts people away from more productive work or leads to environmental degradation. It can no longer be assumed that adequate energy will be available for rural development.

○ *Multiple inputs* Rural development practice (such as that described in the Commission of the European Communities' *Manual for the Preparation and Appraisal of Project Dossiers*) recognizes that most objectives can be achieved only by combining a number of essential inputs, one of which is energy.

○ *Synergy* Many inputs to rural development are not viable on their own, but when combined with other interventions provide enhanced benefits. Energy inputs appear to be particularly valuable in enhancing the benefits of other rural investments.

○ *Location specificity and the need for projects to evolve in response to changes in local conditions* Given the unavoidable uncertainty about the future and the impossibility of knowing everything about a rural location in advance, successful rural development projects do not adopt a rigid plan or 'blueprint', but rather evolve in the light of experience gained through monitoring. Energy supply and demand in particular are known to vary considerably over time and between locations. They therefore need careful action at each location.

○ *Continuity of funding and the utilization of past experience in the energy sector* Recent changes in the aid policy of donors (especially in the policy of Sectoral Concentration under the Lomé III agreement) concentrate resources on rural development and reduce funds from more traditional energy projects. This presents a danger of breaking the continuity of past funding and of dissipating the trust and expertise developed over many years in the energy sector. It is therefore important to harness this expertise and experience in support of the new funding directions such as rural development.

---

[2] The word 'project' is used in this guide as a short-hand expression to describe projects, programmes and all other development activities that are supported by aid agencies.

Chapter 3 provides details of the role energy plays in rural development and highlights the consequences of neglecting energy.

Is energy different from other aspects of rural development?

Conceptually, the provision of energy to a rural development project is no different from the provision of other necessary inputs. Energy comes in many forms and is used for many purposes in the process of social and economic development. Energy is required, for example, to generate shaft power for agricultural and rural industry; for electric lighting in homes, schools and health centres; for heat for cooking and rural industry. These and many other energy requirements are discussed in detail later in the book. In practice, however, the energy dimension has some *unique features* that necessitate special care:

○ Unlike most other inputs, energy is an essential input to *all* rural activity. Energy is so pervasive an ingredient that the design of rural development activity (and the choice of technology) is often based on implicit assumptions about the existing availability of energy. Experience suggests the opposite: that energy supply options should be integrated into each rural development package.

○ Data on rural energy systems has only recently been gathered, and they remain one of the least known elements of the rural economy.

○ The high instability of international oil prices has made the economic appraisal of *all* energy options particularly uncertain.

○ New energy supplies often require large capital expenditures and have longer gestation periods than other infrastructural investments.

How can an energy dimension be added to rural development projects?

Rural energy systems are extremely complex. Unfortunately, for effective development it is simply impossible to avoid these problems. *Energy is not merely an* add-on*, but an essential ingredient for success.* Many actions follow naturally from an awareness of the importance of energy to successful rural development.

Experienced administrators, once they are aware of the importance of energy, and they have an in-depth understanding of local energy-related social, economic and technical factors, will themselves be the most appropriate people within development agencies to specify what precise actions need to be taken into account for energy in the particular rural development activities that they face. *The first task is therefore to create awareness of the key issues.*

3

The key issues

THE DOMINANCE OF WOODFUELS (See also Chapter 3, p. 36–56).

The most important energy sources in rural areas are wood and other biomass fuels. Typically, more than 80 per cent of rural inanimate energy (when measured in energy and not monetary units) comes from biomass, although the importance of wood may be much less in some areas.

Is there or may there be a woodfuel problem?

The problems caused by the shortage of biomass fuels can be severe and have long-term environmental effects. In the short term some groups within rural society, especially poor women, are already suffering considerable hardship as a result of a woodfuel shortage. The precise extent and rate of change of biomass fuel problems in any location can only be determined by site assessment, not just of physical resources but also of the desires of local people.

The causes of deforestation are complex. The main cause is land clearance to produce food or, in some countries, logging for export rather than for local fuel needs. Rural development projects can worsen shortages by changing farming systems. High yielding crop varieties, mechanization, irrigation, and changed cropping patterns may reduce crop residues available as fodder and fuel.

Any rural development project should consider methods for improving woodfuel supply. There are three categories of intervention:

○ plant more trees;

○ reduce household wood use;

○ reduce rural industrial and other wood use.

Can trees be planted?

Simply expanding existing forests is rarely sufficient to increase the supply of wood to those suffering from shortages. Domestic biomass fuels come from many places other than the forest (such as fences, crop residues, roadside trees). Moreover, trees can be incorporated into many projects. They can be planted along roads, within settlements, along field boundaries, or interspaced with crops and around canals and dams, for example. In each of these cases a woodfuel dimension is easily justified:

○ as well as providing fuel, trees give shade, act as a windbreak, and provide fodder for livestock;

4

○ if a serious wood shortage develops, people will not remain at new settlements, but will move elsewhere looking for fuel for cooking;

○ siltation as a consequence of deforestation may reduce the capacity of surface irrigation schemes, and reduce the effective life of hydro-electric dams. Furthermore, if agricultural residues are burnt for fuel, crop yields may fall as soil fertility decreases. The result can be much-reduced benefits from irrigation schemes.

The objective will often be to grow trees for some other purpose, and thus obtain fuelwood as a useful by-product, rather than grow wood for fuel *per se*.

Rural development projects may wish to consider social forestry. This is the planting of trees by the local people for their own use. However, mismanagement of woodland is common and is also likely to affect new forestry projects unless the rural social structures involved are well understood. The private growing of wood by individual farmers is usually easier to organize than community wood growing because ownership rights are more clearly defined. The main issues to consider for a tree project are:

○ What are the trees for?

○ What are the best species, sites, planting and management methods?

○ Who will own the trees?

○ Who will manage the trees?

○ Can the access to the trees by others be controlled?

○ Will the project compete with labour required for other essential activities, especially at peak farming seasons?

Technical solutions alone, such as revolutionary new tree species, are rarely enough. It can take many years to grow trees, and so there is often a long interval between tree planting and the benefits of an enhanced fuel supply. In addition, rural people have many problems other than woodfuel scarcity. Consequently, *social forestry projects are more likely to succeed if they are integrated into, and thereby increase the profitability of, other agricultural projects*, and if trees can provide fodder, poles, and fruit.

Can the amount of wood used by households be reduced?

An alternative to increasing the supply of wood is to reduce fuelwood use. This can be done either by switching to other fuels or by increasing the efficiency of woodfuel use in cooking.

There are severe limits to the extent that modern fuels can be used for

5

cooking in rural areas. Electricity is almost never used for cooking and should not be encouraged.

The consumption of woodfuel can be reduced by showing people how to use cooking fires more efficiently (e.g. by using windshields) or by introducing improved stove designs. Often variations in *per capita* wood consumption between households and regions come about through differences in the effectiveness of fire management. Introducing new designs of stove in rural areas has proven to be far from easy; most rural people do not have spare cash to purchase improved ceramic or metal stoves. If they make their own stoves out of clay, costs are reduced, but it is difficult to distribute design information adequately and to make sure that the stoves are properly made.

The main beneficiaries of improved stoves are women. It is rural women who have to spend hours collecting fuel and cooking in smoke-filled kitchens. All programmes involving women should therefore consider improvements to the rural woodfuel situation in order to release women's time for other, more fruitful activities.

Since deforestation may not be caused by the energy consumption of rural households, introducing new stoves may not reduce the number of trees being cut. Some rural problems may also be best tackled by action in urban areas. Urban households pay cash for wood shipped in from rural areas. An important way of reducing total wood consumption may be to introduce new, more efficient wood stoves or cheap, efficient kerosene stoves in cities. As city dwellers are paying cash for fuel, they can buy metal or ceramic stoves with the money saved by using the more efficient stove. The most successful stoves programmes have usually followed this approach.

Can the effect of rural industries on wood resources be reduced?

Rural industries such as brickmaking, tea drying, fish smoking, and fence construction can be a large drain on wood resources. Charcoal making is also an important rural industry which consumes wood. Charcoal is much lighter than wood with the same heat content and can therefore be shipped to urban areas more economically. Projects that expand these industries in rural areas should consider planting woodland specifically to meet their needs.

Much wood can be saved by encouraging all industries to use the *best practice* for each industry. Conservation programmes are most effective when groups of industries are targeted to increase the impact. Key target groups are agricultural processing, brickworks, and charcoal manufacture.

As woodfuel can be obtained at very low cost, it is often difficult to introduce new, more efficient technologies which require the purchase of expensive equipment. New technologies will not be adopted unless some other benefit can be offered, or unless wood cutting can be controlled in some way.

PETROLEUM PRODUCTS (See also Chapter 3, p. 57–67 and 76–87)

Is the supply of diesel oil sufficient at all times in the year?

Diesel oil often appears to be an important ingredient for increasing agricultural productivity. It is used in stationary diesel engines driving pumps and threshers, for tractors, and for rural transportation. In project planning it is risky to suppose that diesel oil will be continuously available to a rural development project. The official price for diesel may be kept low by subsidies, but this often means that the local oil companies do not put much effort into distributing diesel oil in rural areas, where demands are relatively low, customers are geographically dispersed, and distribution costs are highest. Poor quality roads may also mean that it is impossible to get diesel shipments during certain times of the year.

All proposed projects that will consume diesel oil must take into account the current supply of diesel oil and methods of improving the reliability of supply and energy conservation. Improvements include building new supply depots, purchasing trucks, developing better harbour facilities and coastal shipping, establishing retail outlets, and sometimes getting advice on negotiation of supply contracts.

The viability of agricultural projects will be much reduced if fuel shortages mean that pumps cannot be run at the time when irrigation is needed, if tractors lie idle, if crop treatment cannot be done at harvest time, and if produce cannot be shipped to market towns. Intermittent fuel supply greatly reduces the effectiveness of other key inputs to projects, such as vehicles for supervision, proper maintenance and repair, and the supply of essential materials.

Kerosene is used for lighting, but typically not for cooking. An increase in kerosene use for cooking could decrease wood consumption. However, there will be few areas where incomes are sufficiently high to make this a major solution to household energy problems. If the use of kerosene became widespread for cooking in rural homes there would be a significant increase in total petroleum product consumption in many countries.

If the supply of diesel oil or kerosene is sufficient, is the price reasonable?

If project success depends upon fuel at a specific price, be sure that the rural consumer is not actually charged a much higher price because of poor administration of official price control.

RURAL ELECTRIFICATION (See also Chapter 3, p. 60–72 and 73–87)

Is the supply of electricity sufficient at all times of the year?

Electricity has many uses in rural areas. Electric motors can be used for any activity that requires stationary shaft power, such as irrigation pumps. As

7

electric motors come in small sizes they are the most suitable method for powering refrigerators and other small appliances. Electricity can also be used for household and street lighting. However, *electricity is almost never used for cooking, the major energy need of most rural people.*

Villages can be electrified through connection to the rural electric grid, or through decentralized electricity generation. There is little evidence to suggest that electricity will by itself lead to rural development. The actual use of electricity depends upon many factors including the availability and reliability of appliances at costs affordable to rural people. Simply because a village is connected to the grid does not mean that electricity will be available when it is needed. Power cuts are common, and worse, surges damage electronic components and bulbs, and low voltages can burn out electric motors. In some areas farmers install electric motors because they are cheap and electricity is subsidized, but they also purchase back-up diesel engines to increase reliability of supply.

Any project that will require electricity and that intends to utilize the electric grid must make sure that the supply of electricity is sufficiently reliable. This may involve investments in electricity transmission and distribution.

If decentralized electricity generation is to be installed, the generation equipment must be reliable. If this is done with diesel generators, then the diesel oil supply must also be sufficiently reliable.

Administering payment for electricity in village electrification schemes is often a problem; the users cannot afford the full cost of supply, and aid agencies and central government are often unwilling to meet recurrent costs on a long-term basis.

NEW AND RENEWABLE ENERGY TECHNOLOGIES (See also p. 80–87.)

There are alternative energy sources to the conventional options of diesel engines and connection to the rural grid. These alternatives are usually most suitable for generating electricity or for producing stationary shaft power. *Their suitability depends upon local conditions and few generalizations are possible.* They are most successful where diesel is difficult to obtain or where grid electricity is not available. There have been sufficient failures of projects that have attempted to introduce these technologies to commend both caution and a careful assessment of local resources, and most importantly the needs of local people.

The most fundamental comment to make with respect to renewable energy technologies is: *do not try experimental technologies. Only use equipment which is known to be reliable in rural environments.* If you must try experiments, expect problems and plan to keep a skilled maintenance team in place for the complete life of the equipment that is installed. The Third World is littered with abandoned technologies that were intended as the solution to rural energy constraints.

Where can renewable energy technologies be used?

An assessment of the complete range of energy options is needed for each location. However, some general comments can be made (see also Chapter 3 and Annexe II).

Photovoltaic arrays Photovoltaic systems produce electricity directly from sunlight. They have very high capital costs, but because they can be made with very small capacities of only a few watts and have low running costs they can be competitive with diesel generators when very small demands for electricity exist. Examples are remote telecommunications, medical refrigerators, and battery charging for lighting and radios.

Windmills Again the capital costs are high. Because of the wide fluctuation of windspeed they are best when used to pump water into a storage tank. For pumping water directly onto crops a very large windmill may be needed to ensure that minimum crop irrigation requirements can be met at key months in the year. Windmills are most appropriate when used for village water supply or the provison of drinking water for animals. Small windmills can also be used to charge batteries.

Water turbines Where a suitable water supply is available, the use of water turbines can be attractive. The simplest application is to use the turbines to power small crop processors such as mills, grinders, and oil expellers (a method that has been widely used for centuries). On a larger scale they can be used to power electric generators for village electrification.

Biogas plants If a farmer owns at least four cattle (but usually more) and they are kept in cattle sheds, the dung from the animals can effectively be used in a biogas plant. The gas produced can be used for domestic cooking, or as a substitute for diesel oil in an engine. As most cattle sheds are close to the house rather than in the fields, nearly all biogas plants have been built to supply household fuel. The capital costs can be high with the result that they are only suitable for wealthier farmers.

The option of using biogas plants to fuel a diesel engine is technically feasible. However, unless the fields are close to the biogas plant, the biogas-fuelled engine cannot be used for irrigation, although it can be used for threshing and other tasks. This would usually yield only modest diesel oil savings.

The faeces of other animals (e.g. pigs) and that of the rural population itself can also be used in a biogas plant. The use of human excreta can be co-ordinated with programmes of village sanitation. However, there are often taboos against cooking with gas derived from human faeces. The use of widely dispersed inputs (e.g. the dung of grazing cattle) and other biomass (e.g. water hyacinth) tends to be problematic, as estimates of the supply of inputs are often over-optimistic.

Gasifiers The conversion of wood into producer gas with a gasifier is another possible subsitute for diesel oil, and one of the few renewable energy options that can be made mobile. At small capacities charcoal must be used as the fuel: tars in the producer gas when wood is gasified can damage the engine unless elaborate and expensive cleaning of the gas is done. For larger engines, filters can be installed to remove volatile liquids from the producer gas. Then wood and some other biomass fuels can be used directly.

The operation of a gasifier requires skilled staff. When wood or charcoal is used as the fuel, the attractiveness of a gasifer depends upon the local woodfuel supply. It is most appropriate for direct heat for crop drying (e.g. tea and coffee) and possibly for decentralized electricity generation, or for industrial engines in remote forest areas (e.g. at sawmills and coffee plantations), but only if there are skilled mechanics and tradespeople available to repair the system.

Can the project support new technologies?

Renewable energy technologies use an energy source that is locally available in the rural environment. This reduces some of the problems of uncertain supplies of diesel oil and electricity, but it must also be recognized that some of the renewable energy sources are inherently variable (e.g. wind, river flow, biomass) or may be already used by someone. Moreover, the problems of maintaining and repairing renewable energy equipment are almost always greater than with conventional systems. *Links to the modern sector for the supply of spare parts will be just as vital as a reliable diesel oil supply is for diesel engines.* This is of particular importance in regions where the local people do not yet have the technical capabilities to repair the new technology by themselves.

Some renewable energy technologies are economic in some locations, even during periods of low oil prices. They deserve serious consideration, but in most situations will have a secondary place to the conventional options of diesel oil and electricity.

Energy project planning

Once the need for an energy dimension is recognized, the next step involves detailed project planning (see also Chapter 2, p. 18–22 and Chapter 3, p. 25–8 and 31–6).

What are the energy needs of rural people?

The needs for energy and also the supply options are site specific. In order to assess the true energy needs of the rural population, proper local consultation is essential. Projects must also respond to any changes in the local environment or to mis-specifications by project planners. Therefore, they must contain regular monitoring and evaluation. Genuine participation by local people in project management, or at least continual consultation, is a key to success.

Different groups in the rural society may have conflicting goals. An understanding of the relationships between different social groups is crucial for community-level projects such as village water supply, village woodland, and decentralized village electrification. Effective participation and consultation is far from a trivial activity. Time, money and expertise must be allowed for this in project planning.

If project benefits are to be sustainable they must meet a real need of the participants, not merely the needs perceived by external agencies. Moreover, subsidy will be necessary if the project meets a need which the rural population cannot afford at their current income levels. *Most energy supply projects also require investment in energy-consuming appliances (i.e. the need for energy is a derived need). Unless the potential energy customers have the financial resources to buy these appliances, no energy will be purchased or used.* This is commonly a problem with rural electrification schemes, where there is often very low demand for many years.

The rural economy is often highly distorted by a range of price subsidies on both agricultural produce and energy. Furthermore, wood can often be collected freely from common land without heed to the cost of growing it. This means the cost of woodfuels does not reflect their replacement cost of their 'true value' to society.

The rural 'price environment' restricts the energy options open to the rural development project manager. A range of pricing adjustments may have a major effect on the feasibility of energy projects and on rural development. The project planner should consider what parts of the 'policy environment' can and cannot be changed.

What resources are there in the location?

Many energy projects must draw on local resources. The most obvious examples are woodfuel projects that require land. Nearly all projects will require some labour and capital inputs from rural people. In general, the greater the commitment of resources by the local population, the greater the chances for success. Moreover, the mobilization of rural resources reduces the need for central government expenditure. This can only happen if an interest in the project is generated in advance of actual implementation.

Project designers must understand not only the current rural energy situation but also how it is changing before they can properly assess the impacts of their intervention. This is difficult to cater for during planning as projects must be formulated within certain time limits and there is very little information on the fuel supply more than a few years ago. However, surveys can be designed for rapid investigation of current trends.

Renewable energy technologies also draw on the local environment, for wind, river flow, or biomass. The feasibility of these technologies is very site specific. A careful assessment of the availability of the relevant energy source for each installation is essential.

Who will implement the project?

Rural energy projects are often difficult to organize because they are not the clear responsibility of any one agency within the recipient state. The agricultural ministry is the government agency most commonly responsible for rural development activities. However, the staff of the agricultural ministry cannot be expected to have the technical knowledge needed to understand the full range of the different energy supply options. On the other hand, the energy ministry with the main responsibility for managing energy projects often has an urban bias in its activities, and a very limited capability to implement projects in rural areas.

Rural energy requires a special kind of energy project, often small scale and geographically dispersed. A different approach may be needed in each location depending upon local conditions. Consequently, current organizational structures may need to be adapted to deal with this scope of work. The methodology of Integrated Rural Development (IRD), popular in the 1970s, has been found to have many difficulties as an approach to development. The integration of energy and development proposed here is quite different in nature. It does not require the large-scale projects that were often a feature of IRD.

An important part of any rural energy project is personnel planning. There is a need for specific re-training of staff. As detailed local assessments may be needed, it is often better to use specialist teams for rural energy projects rather than simply adding to the knowledge of already overburdened agricultural extension workers. However, the intervention of specialist teams may only have a short-term influence, while the slower approach of training extension workers can have a long-term impact.

The needs for local repair and maintenance facilities are frequently understated. Energy is only consumed if appliances are used, and the consumer can keep them running. Even if a good and reliable supply of diesel oil or electricity is introduced into an area, it does not automatically follow that there will be any change in the behaviour of the local people.

The actions available to the administrator to implement energy planning are described in Chapter 2, and Chapter 3 provides a more detailed explanation of the key issues associated with energy in the context of rural development.

2 The administrative options

What can be done

At the outset it is important to recognize the limits of administrative action — what can't be done.

- ○ It is not possible to provide a simple formula to decide which energy technologies are better than others — it all depends on specific needs and precise local conditions. There is no substitute for good local knowledge and this knowledge can seldom be gained quickly or cheaply.

- ○ Technical solutions are rarely sufficient on their own to achieve rural development — beware the advocate of the single technical solution who is looking for a problem to solve.

- ○ Project aid is usually unable to remove major constraints to development (such as the distribution of land holdings) or to influence the macro policies of a country (such as agricultural or energy prices).

- ○ It is rarely possible to build adequate local capability or local institutions during the span of a single project (typically three years) — such tasks are crucial but require long-term commitment.

- ○ Energy inputs in support of rural people frequently require recurrent expenditure. It is rarely possible to sustain aid support for recurrent expenditure for more than a few years.

- ○ It cannot be assumed that existing staff will have time to undertake new tasks and responsibilities without abandoning some other task.

The range of possible administrative action can be divided as follows:

- ○ at the level of the institution;
- ○ at the level of macro policies for a nation;
- ○ at the level of an individual project or programme.

The range of administrative action will also vary between locations:

- ○ actions for donors;
- ○ actions for recipients.

13

While the most immediate action is likely to be possible only at the project level, greater effect will be achieved by action at the national and institutional level. Generally, concern for energy will involve:

○ providing institutional mechanisms and a policy environment in which energy is given sufficient weight in rural projects;

○ insisting that consultants and project designers take energy into account in their thinking and in their proposals;

○ providing the finance, skills and time necessary to incorporate energy into rural activities;

○ assisting in the clarification of objectives, ensuring that a full range of options is considered and, where necessary, bringing together the skills and advice of knowledgeable people.

Action at the institutional level

The key institutional problem for a development agency is to design administrative procedures that encourage consideration of the energy dimension. This will require not only asking the right questions about the type of energy intervention that is necessary for each rural development activity, but also ensuring that the right answers are properly implemented. The discussion in the chapter is focused primarily on institutional options within donor agencies, but similar issues relate to national agencies responsible for rural development. Action is required in five areas:

○ responsibility;

○ capability;

○ awareness;

○ procedures;

○ documentation.

Responsibility

Experience in a number of countries suggests that one of the major constraints to energy planning is that the agencies most able to take action in rural areas (usually the Departments of Agriculture, Rural Development, Irrigation and Forestry) have little or no knowledge about energy, while the agencies most knowledgeable about energy (the Ministry of Energy, the electricity utility and the petroleum supply companies) have little capability for action in rural areas.

Similar constraints operate within donor organizations. Energy departments have traditionally built up experience of modern energy supplies (most notably electricity generation and transmission) and have little knowledge of rural realities or contact with rural implementing agencies.

Effective action to overcome this constraint will depend on the particular local conditions but, in general, action might include:

○ appointing an individual or group with clear responsibility for energy issues within the departments responsible for rural implementation. A strong example is when energy personnel are placed in the offices responsible for rural development activities, and thus work alongside rural development staff.

○ serious efforts at liaison between the Departments of Energy and Rural Policy & Implementation — such activities have to be effectively encouraged by the donor's representative within the recipient country, particularly at the early stage of project/programme identification.

○ within recipient countries the strong participation of Planning and Budget or similar ministries with the potential of bridging the rural policy and energy authorities.

Capability for energy planning

Within institutions involved with the identification and planning of rural development activities, it is unlikely to be possible to include people with expertise on every detail of energy and its conversion technologies. What is required above all else is an individual (or group forming a specialist Energy Unit) with the ability to identify the energy problem associated with rural development and make choices between options. Such an individual or Unit would need the knowledge of when and where to go for more specialist information (a start to this process is provided in Chapter 3 and Annexe II).

It would also be important for the Energy Unit to develop systematically a knowledge of which consultants, contractors and other people involved with the implementation of rural activities were capable of responding to rural situations with effective energy programmes. Individuals and contracting firms might be encouraged by administrators to develop their own energy response by including such capabilities within terms of reference and invitations to tender (see p. 17). However, experience suggests that foreign consultants and contractors are not well suited to implementing many types of rural energy project. This is particularly so where each individual installation is small in size, where there are many such installations spread over a wide geographical area, and where local knowledge is an important element in the acceptability and viability of the investment.

In addition to developing knowledge about the capability of people, it would also be important for the Energy Unit to develop systematically a knowledge of the range of energy interventions and the policy options. This book provides a first indication of the technical options, but the Energy Unit needs to build up its knowledge of the performance under local conditions of the equipment considered.

Such knowledge comes in part from effective monitoring of on-going activities; the systematic recording of the characteristics and local performance of equipment arising from these monitoring activities, possibly in the form of a computerized data base; and the adoption of equipment standards. Standards are particularly important where it is intended that decentralized energy projects are to be subsequently connected to the electric grid. But they are also important for equipment that is frequently used in rural development projects.

Awareness of the energy dimension

The persistent task of energy units is to create an awareness of the energy dimension within agencies planning and implementing activities in rural areas. Rural specialists will often know what is the most appropriate energy action for their particular circumstances once they recognize the importance of energy in their activities.

This awareness can be fostered by a number of actions:

○ the explicit monitoring of the energy elements of rural development projects and the feeding back of this experience into future policy and procedures;

○ specific attempts to seek out and publicize examples of both success and failure in taking account of energy in rural development activities;

○ the inclusion of energy issues in the on-going training programmes of rural departments;

○ the inclusion of energy issues in office procedures (see p. 18).

Procedures and standard terms of reference

Institutions involved with rural development (both donors and recipients) should review their procedures to see whether these need to be adapted to ensure an adequate assessment of energy implications. However, the most important actions occur at the earliest stages of the project cycle*:

---

* The 'project cycle' conventionally consists of: 1. identification; 2. feasibility; 3. design; 4. *ex ante* appraisal; 5. approval; 6. implementation (including monitoring/feedback/adaptation); 7. operation (including monitoring/feedback/adaptation); 8. *ex post* evaluation.

identification, and the feasibility testing of the various options. Often these stages are most difficult to organize and adapt.

The first procedural step will be to *decide which proposals to finance rural projects could and should be examined by the Energy Unit* (or energy adviser) within the institution. In many cases, such as that of the Commission of the European Communities (CEC), Financing Proposals are not required to be approved by energy specialists. Indeed there are not enough energy specialists even to examine all energy projects, let alone all rural projects. Their influence can only be that of persuasion, and their strategy must be to identify points at which their influence is most effective and to identify in advance those projects most likely to include an energy dimension.

A system for identifying in advance which projects are likely to require energy planning might include:

○ projects that use considerable inputs of inanimate energy (e.g. agricultural mechanization, pumped irrigation, rural transport);

○ projects that are highly dependent on small but secure supplies of energy (e.g. medical supplies, telecommunications, etc);

○ projects that are known to have large indirect effects on the local energy system (land clearance, projects involving changes in land use, projects involving changes in cooking practices, projects increasing the density of populations).

Apart from creating a general sense of awareness about energy, the administrator's most powerful instrument is the design of terms of reference. Consideration should be given to inclusion of the following *standard terms of reference* in all contracts concerned with the identification, design, feasibility testing and *ex ante* appraisal studies of rural activities:

○ 'the consultant/contractor/project designer should examine how robust the proposal/project/programme for rural development is to changes in the cost and/or availability of energy supplies;

○ 'the consultant/contractor/project designer should examine whether the value/profitability/sustainability/impact of the proposal can be increased by the addition of investments to improve or secure an adequate energy supply';

○ 'the consultant/contractor/project designer should examine whether indirect effects are likely to arise from the project which will affect the local energy situation'.

Consideration might also be given to *requiring that standard energy-related investments should be added to all rural development activities* (such as the inclusion of rural electrification to all area development schemes over a certain size). The onus of proof would then be transferred to those proposing projects to show why such investments should not be included rather than proof than they should. Such an approach may prove controversial, however.

In terms of institutional procedures, experience with energy aid in the past suggests that it is important to *clarify what is meant by experimental, pilot and demonstration projects.* Such terms are frequently used to avoid compliance with the conventional criteria for project approval (such as providing an adequate economic rate of return). To qualify as this type of project, the activity should be novel, replicable, carefully monitored, and the experience of the project should be adequately recorded and fed back into administrative procedures. Demonstration projects should be the first stage of a process of commercialization.

Inclusion of energy issues in project documentation

An extension of procedural changes is to adapt the documentation required at the various stages of the project cycle to take account of the energy dimension. As a minimum it seems likely that the document on the basis of which a decision is made to finance an activity should include a section on the energy aspects (in the European Development Fund this would be the *Financing Proposal*). This might take a form similar to the requirements of many agencies to demonstrate that concerns about women and the environment have been adequately taken into account in project planning.

○ 'the Financing Proposal should indicate how robust the proposal/ project/programme for rural development is to changes in the cost and/or availability of energy supplies';

○ 'the Financing Proposal should indicate whether the value/ profitability/sustainability/impact of a particular proposal can be increased by the addition of investments to improve or secure an adequate energy supply';

○ 'the Financing Proposal should indicate whether indirect effects are likely to arise from the project which will affect local energy needs (particularly for electricity, fossil fuels, or woodfuels)'.

Many agencies and development institutions have manuals and guidelines for the preparation of project propsals (in the CEC it is *The Manual for Preparing and Appraising Project Dossiers — VIII/527/79/rev2.85*). It is important not only that these have an adequate set of *guiding principles* covering energy projects, but that all sections dealing with rural development include reminders of the need to consider energy.

Action at the level of macro policy

Administrators will be able to take into account energy needs most easily at the level of their own institution or at the level of individual projects. However, projects and programmes for rural development operate within the economic conditions of the country and within the policies set by the State. *This 'macro policy environment' strongly influences the feasibility of energy interventions.*

The main features of this environment which affect energy planning are described in Chapter 3 and include:

○ the laws and administrative rules setting out how state and private energy enterprises operate (such as the power utility or the oil supply companies);

○ the terms of trade between rural and urban people (which determine how much money rural people have to buy equipment and fuel supplied by urban people);

○ policies to extend the electricity grid to particular rural areas, or to improve the transport of fuels to rural areas (this determines many of the energy options available);

○ energy pricing policy (if electricity and kerosene are subsidized it is difficult for other unsubsidized energy options to compete);

○ the system of taxes and subsidies — technologies which are eligible for subsidy may diffuse more quickly than those that are not;

○ credit policy — the allocation of credit to particular social groups or to particular rural activities influences what energy technology is viable and alters the specific energy needs of rural people.

The sustainability of a rural energy project over a number of years will often depend on the competition from other energy sources. This competition is itself determined by the 'macro policy environment'. For instance, it is not usually possible to introduce at their full cost alternative energy sources to assist pumped irrigation in areas where electricity from the grid is provided at tariffs that are below the cost of electricity generation.

Attempts to influence this 'macro policy environment' are legitimate activities of domestic energy agencies and foreign aid donors. With donors, such attempts to alter macro policies take the form of 'development dialogue' (at best) and the imposition of 'conditionality clauses' in aid agreements (at worst). Within the European Development Fund, the main possibilities for introducing policy changes at the macro level occur during the programming missions that define the future collaboration under each Lomé Agreement.

The key issue here is to determine whether there are elements in macro policy which provide a barrier to dealing effectively with energy in rural development. Such barriers might be identified as part of the preparations for programming missions by local or foreign consultants.

Frequently donors press for energy-pricing policies that reflect the cost of supply (technically the 'long-run marginal cost'). However, it is difficult to provide general guidance on this matter. Many of the objectives of low-cost energy can be met more effectively by subsidies to the energy conservation technology (e.g. electric motors, biogas plant) than by subsidies to the price of energy. Donors also press for low interest or grant aid funds to be lent on to local institutions at realistic rates of interest to encourage proper financial control.

Donors can also encourage the effective liaison (described on page 15) between the institutions involved with rural development and those that have the expertise about energy matters. Within rural development agencies, attempts to influence the macro policy environment are part of the on-going process of policy making and review.

It is one of the tasks of energy units within government to undertake reviews (possibly with the assistance of local or foreign expertise) to determine how current and proposed policies directly (or more often indirectly) affect energy developments within the rural areas.

More generally it is important (but in reality quite difficult) for energy units to press for policy changes that would more effectively build local capacities to provide effective energy interventions in rural development. Such efforts might be included in:

○ national policies for training;

○ policies governing the import of energy technology;

○ policies to encourage small-scale industry in rural areas;

○ policies for forest development.

The energy dimension at the level of projects and programmes

Many of the actions identified above at the institutional level can be applied on an *ad hoc* basis to individual projects. A number of specific actions are identified in the Annexes. The key actions are:

○ to encourage the *identification of energy inputs* and consequences at an early stage of the project cycle so that they can be integrated into project design at the outset (possibly by requesting information on current and expected energy use in the project area);

○ to encourage the *consideration of a wide range of technical and other options* at an early stage of project design;

○ to *insert the three standard terms of reference* into all contracts and job descriptions (see p. 17);

○ to include the energy dimension in the *documentation* supporting a proposal to finance a project (see p. 18).

Seven key factors for project success

Experience suggests that the success of rural energy projects depends on seven key factors.

1. The project meets the energy needs of users

The energy needs of rural people are intimately linked to their social, economic and political lives; they will vary greatly between different social groups and between different locations. The need for energy may not be matched by a willingness or ability to pay for the energy (this is the difference between a need and an effective demand). Energy demands are a derived demand, meaning that people require energy to do something else that they want — for lighting, or motive power to pump water — rather than energy *per se*.

○ *Action*: determine which energy needs are important to the success of the rural development scheme. If in doubt, seek the opinion of an energy specialist at the earliest possibility.

○ *Action*: ensure that each social group (including women) is genuinely consulted and their opinions understood. Beware of mathematical models purporting to indicate energy needs, particularly if they do not include new data gathered from the project site.

○ *Action*: ensure that energy supply is linked to the likely availability of energy-using appliances and energy conversion devices.

2. Energy interventions are carefully designed in relation to specific local conditions

Ex post aid evaluations suggest that small rural energy projects require careful design just as much as large energy projects. Their economic and technical viability is highly dependent on local conditions.

○ *Action*: ensure the allocation of necessary time, finance and expertise to achieve careful design by people who know the operating environment.

○ *Action*: ensure long-term commitment to meeting energy needs by aid agencies and local institutions so that the necessary infrastructure can be built up and local people trained.

3. The energy intervention produces a cash benefit

Most of the rural energy system is outside the cash economy. Therefore interventions which require people to invest cash have to compete with non-cash options (such as stealing fuelwood). Many energy interventions require recurrent expenditure of cash to sustain them (for instance to buy fuel and spare parts). Energy projects must also pay for lost productivity from the re-assignment of resources necessary to use the energy supply.

○ *Action*: check who pays both for initial and for recurrent costs. If the project does not directly generate recurrent cash benefits, see if energy investment for one purpose (e.g. rural lighting) can be paid for out of earnings from its use for another (e.g. use micro-hydro to provide electricity and grain milling) and/or secure initial and recurrent costs through reliable public sector sources.

4. Costs of energy intervention must be in proportion to income levels (poverty) of local users

Even if the financial and economic returns on an energy intervention are high, the absolute amount of the required investment may exceed the cash-flow resources of individual users. Providing energy equipment free of charge to users may not induce sufficient commitment for the proper use and maintenance of the equipment.

○ *Action*: ensure project designers have knowledge of the local situation and consider options appropriate to local cash availability.

○ *Action*: for projects where the donor provides energy-producing equipment free to the rural community, consider requiring a contribution (fixed one-off payment, fixed monthly amount, fixed percentage of initial cost, etc.) which the community or beneficiaries must contribute to a maintenance fund for the equipment.

5. Technical interventions are appropriate to local conditions and local needs

Technical options should be adaptable to a wide range of changes to local conditions. Technical options should be known to be reliable in the rural setting; if they are experimental, they should be tested on a pilot basis together with effective monitoring, evaluation and feedback to record how effective the technology is in the particular application.

○ *Action*: check that a wide range of technical options was considered and why the chosen option was selected.

○ *Action*: beware of untried technology — check what evidence there is that the technology has operated successfully in similar conditions.

○ *Action*; if the technology is experimental, ensure that there are effective procedures for recording and evaluating the experience. Check that donor support, if applicable, includes the full costs of such evaluation.

6. Sufficient capability to design, supply, install, operate, maintain and repair energy technologies

Ex-post evaluations of energy aid suggest that the local capabilities to undertake all the processes in the project cycle effectively are rarely available for small-scale rural energy projects. Furthermore, such skills cannot easily be imported from overseas (e.g. by hiring consultants). However, such capabilities are essential for success and long-term viability. The development of such capability should therefore be a central objective of energy planning.

○ *Action*: check that necessary capacities have been determined and are *genuinely* available. Where gaps are found, ensure that sufficient funds and time are made available to develop the necessary local capability as part of the project. This is not an expensive luxury, but an essential input to ensure the viability of a rural development activity.

7. Activities must be honestly monitored, and technology, project design and associated institutions should be adapted in the light of the knowledge gained

Ex-post evaluations show that institutions and aid agencies have some reluctance to monitor their activities and to report problems in such a way that the necessary changes can be made in the light of this knowledge. Donor agencies, local administrators and politicians appear often to want to hear only the good news.

But since rural societies are complex and preliminary information-gathering is inevitably inadequate, such adaptive (or evolutionary) behaviour is the only strategy likely to remain viable.

○ *Action*: Wherever possible, arrange an *ex-post* evaluation by a competent but disinterested party.

3 Energy in the context of rural development

In this chapter the issues outlined in Chapters 1 and 2 are examined in more detail. Initially some general issues relating to energy and rural development are discussed. While this may be common ground to the administrators of rural development projects, it is useful to define the general approach. In this section we review agricultural policies, rural financial institutions, and the evolution of rural development strategies.

The second section of the chapter discusses traditional energy and rural development. While traditional energy sources include people and animals, the focus here is on the use of wood and other biomass fuels. These are used for cooking, and by a range of rural industries. This is followed by a review of policy interventions to improve the rural woodfuel situation. These fall in two broad categories: forestry programmes to increase wood supply, and stove programmes to decrease wood consumption.

The third section discusses the transfer from traditional fuel to modern forms of energy such as petroleum products, electricity, or advanced renewable energy technologies. It examines the possibility of using kerosene as a household fuel, and the energy requirements of agricultural mechanization, rural industries, and social projects. This is followed with a review of energy supply options including rural electrification and a range of renewable energy technologies, and concludes with some brief comments on the choice of energy project for the development of rural activities.

The rural se⌄ior and the dynamics of development

The vast majority of poor people in developing countries are to be found in rural areas. They often live on the barest of means, and have to rely on the scarce resources within their environment to meet their basic needs. In some countries, notably in Latin America, poverty will become more of an urban phenomenon in the future, paralleling a similar shift in poverty during the early stages of industrialization in many European countries. However, for most countries the population of rural poor will remain large for the foreseeable future.

Donor agencies and other international organizations have increasingly given their support to rural development policies in developing countries in an attempt to ameliorate the unequal distribution of economic growth between urban and rural areas. In the main, these new assistance policies

24

reflect a shift away from the traditional method of achieving growth through urban industrialization, towards directly improving agricultural productivity and the quality of rural life. Most aid agencies and governments are now agreed that equitable growth cannot be attained through a 'trickle-down' from urban-based industrial growth, and it is argued that the economic growth of the last few decades has done little to better the condition of the vast majority of poor people in developing countries. Indeed the nature of growth is often said to have exacerbated their problems (Rondinelli and Ruddle, 1978, p. 487). Improving the quality of rural life, it is further argued, will help to stem the unmanageable migration of rural people to urban squalor.

Agriculture is the main source of livelihood for most rural dwellers. The poor include small farmers and landless labourers, with households headed by women among the most desperate cases. Illiteracy, unemployment and underemployment, disease and high mortality rates are all characteristics of life for many in rural areas. Not only are incomes and the ownership of assets, particularly land, unequally distributed, but often the better-off rural elites have control over the better quality assets. Consequently, the costs of reaching the neediest sections of society with basic services such as health care, employment training and drinking water are often high.

Energy supply is one essential dimension to rural development

The purpose of this section is to set the role of energy in the context of development strategies. The need to consider energy in rural development is highlighted by the estimates of the Office of Energy of the United States Agency for International Development that some $100 million in agricultural output was lost in Sudan in 1984 owing to shortage of approximately $16 million worth of energy supplies for irrigation and tillage; while in Somalia lack of diesel fuel was reported to have reduced irrigated crop output by 40 to 60 per cent in the same year (Office of Energy, 1986; quoted by Jones, 1988, p. 1). An understanding of the organization of development projects is important if an energy component is to be successfully integrated.

Agricultural policies

There are many biases against rural people, a major example being agricultural pricing policies: this is done for the benefit of urban consumers

In most developing countries there are strong political and economic biases against rural areas and toward urban areas (see Bates, 1981; Lipton, 1977). Examples of this are policies that hold the prices of agricultural produce well below their economic value. Pressures for this action come from a variety of sources. (See Michailof, 1987, p. 35.) Firstly, the urban work-

25

force is usually very concerned by inflationary erosion of their wages. Urban workers are also normally in a position of relatively strong political power. Numerous attempts have been made by many governments to increase the prices of different commodities, food and energy among the most common, only to have to back down in the face of urban rioting.

Agricultural policies are usually derived from other policy goals: sometimes they help the rural poor, but more often not

'Even at the risk of being provocative, we could almost say that the success of agricultural development policies and projects undertaken throughout the world to attack rural poverty is independent of the political situation [ranging on a horizontal axis from conservative to so-called revolutionary regimes]. On the other hand, this success is far from independent of the position of these operations on a vertical axis, at the top of which a model of the participative type would be placed, and at the bottom of which a totally bureaucratic model would be found'. (Michailof, 1987, p. 79)

Many agricultural policies are derived from other policy goals (Bates, 1981). In some cases this can work in the favour of rural people; for example, businesses involved in transportation may lobby for subsidized diesel oil, which can also be used by farmers. Similarly a subsidy on kerosene for urban households is usually a subsidy for all kerosene consumers, be they urban or rural. The most pervasive pricing policy, however, is the attempt to keep the price of agricultural commodities as low as possible, effectively taxing farmers in order to appease urban workers and employers. The extent to which this is a tax on the very poor depends upon the nature of the poor's involvement in agriculture. For landless labourers, cheap foodstuffs are offset by a reduced demand for their labour resulting from suppressed agricultural production. Other biases against public investment in rural areas towards towns and cities come from the same sources.

Agricultural prices can be controlled by official marketing boards, or through over-valued exchange rates

Different methods can be used to reduce agricultural prices. The most direct is to have official marketing boards that are the only permitted purchasers of agricultural produce (i.e. legalized 'monopsonies'). These organizations can then offer farmers lower prices for their products, although this need not necessarily be the case (see Giri, 1986, p. 67–72).

As a result of these policies, the farmgate price of commodities is often well below their economic value. For example, the World Bank (1986) notes:

'In Ethiopia . . . farmgate procurement prices have been far below the import parity prices; in 1985, for instance, the import parity prices (at the official exchange rate) for maize, sorghum, and wheat were respectively about 80 per cent, 50 per cent, and 45 per cent above the farmgate prices . . . the maize procurement price in Tanzania was only a quarter of the border price. In Cameroon, Ghana, and Tanzania, rice producers were paid only about half the border price'(p. 6).

The degree to which farmers actually sell at these prices depends upon the country and the region. Controls on trade of this type are the natural domain of the corrupt official. Marketing boards, for example, may receive only a small proportion of the goods intended for them, the remainder being smuggled. Perhaps only 10 to 30 per cent of the foodstuffs intended for marketing boards actually goes through them (Bates, 1981, p. 40; Giri, 1986, p. 73).

International aid often requires a reduction of these controls in order to help the rural poor, but more needs to be done

This distortion of the economy against the poor has led many international development organizations, including the European Commission, to call for a radical change in agricultural pricing policies and the dismantling of state marketing boards. However, some reports do not go much further with their policy prognosis. The World Bank, for example, suggested in 1986 that raising agricultural prices (up to international levels) comes close to being a sufficient condition for agricultural development (Michailof, 1987, p. 97).

Simply adjusting prices may be necessary, but is far from being sufficient for agricultural development (see also Michailof, 1987, p. 97). The notable exception to this occurs when there is a major new agricultural technology on the margin of profitability under existing prices; i.e. when a modest increase in prices permits radically different farming systems (one example of this is hybrid maize in parts of Zimbabwe; see Lipton, 1987). Other biases against agriculture include inadequate spending on public health, education, and farm input delivery systems. Under these circumstances farm output cannot be expected to respond significantly to price increases without addressing these shortcomings. To quote Lipton:

'. . . major public sector actions are needed to enable farmers to respond to prices by significantly raising total output. These actions are . . . (i) to render work healthier and less strenuous . . .; (ii) to reduce the risks of output expansion, e.g. by supporting micro-irrigation; (iii) to stimulate appropriate agricultural research; and (iv) to raise the poorest people's purchasing power over food. Experiences in Taiwan and the Indian Punjab, and elsewhere, . . . show that only if governments do more in such ways, in and for agriculture (and improve poor farm households' access to credit), can they expect a substantial response of total farm output when they do less to repress farm prices' (1987, p. 203).

Biases exist against the provision of energy to rural people

Similar arguments are made by Streeten (1987). The supply of energy needed to improve agricultural productivity clearly falls in this same category, and it is not surprising that biases in the provision of energy also exist in many countries. These take several forms, including direct investments in supply infrastructure by national companies, and energy-pricing policies which encourage supply companies to ignore rural markets.

The petroleum products most commonly used in rural areas are often subsidized. Although this benefits rural consumers, it much reduces the financial profitability of investing in distribution networks, and the end effect can be that oil companies do not market their petroleum products in rural areas. Oil products are simply not available at the subsidized price.

The limited purchasing power of rural populations can also lead to the direct transfer of resources from villages and farms to cities and towns. A common example is the displacement of rural people by hydro-power dams, with households adjacent to the dam having no access to the electricity generated. Fuelwoods can also be trucked considerable distances from rural areas, where it can be almost free for the truckers, to cities where consumers will pay cash for wood.

Rural financial institutions

Credit is needed to buy new equipment, but this can be expensive unless rural financial institutions are established

One attempt to remedy the bias against the rural sector resulting from low crop prices and government investment policies has been the creation of institutions offering subsidized credit to farmers. Indeed, in the 1960s and 1970s subsidized rural credit was seen as one of the main answers to the problem of rural development. This resulted from the observation that the availability of credit from traditional informal sources — from the local moneylender, from friends and relatives, and from landowners to sharecroppers and tenants — were at usurious and exploitative rates. Surveys of informal lending practices in rural areas give a median interest rate of 50 per cent per annum (Braverman and Gausch, 1986). Many of the energy technologies we will discuss in subsequent sections involve the purchase of equipment, and as with other rural development projects the need for credit must be addressed.

These rural financial institutions need not offer subsidized credit

The consensus regarding the effectiveness of subsidized rural credit is changing, and it is argued that cheap loans do not appear to increase agricultural production, do not encourage the investment in new technology, and particularly do not reach the poor (see, for example, Adams *et al.*, 1984; Adams and Graham, 1981; Donald, 1976; Von Pischke *et al.*, 1983). Both the subsidized credit itself and the institutions responsible for distributing rural credit are blamed for this lack of satisfactory performance (Adams and Vogel, 1986; Braverman and Gausch, 1986).

Subsidized credit reduces saving by rural people and rarely reaches the poor

The main argument against subsidized credit itself is that it tends to suppress rural savings. In defence of subsidized credit it is argued that the rural poor are so poor that they have no margin for saving anyway, and as a result they do not respond to higher interest rates. Having to offer savers high interest deposits will merely drive rural credit institutions into bankruptcy, and drive funds into urban areas. The counter argument is that even the poorest people hold some liquid assets to cope with emergencies and, by being forced to hold cash, are being forced to pay an inflation tax. It is further noted that some of the most successful rural credit schemes have been those that have mobilized local savings. A classical example is that of Korea, where the proportion of loans covered by savers' deposits grew from 20 per cent in 1961 to more than 50 per cent in 1975. At the same time, participation by farmers grew to some 80 per cent (Braverman and Gausch, p.1258; see also the case of Nicaragua in Von Pischke *et al.*, 1983; Lipton, 1981).

More important criticisms centre on the institutional problems found with most rural credit schemes. One of the major complaints against subsidized credit is that most of it goes to the relatively wealthy sections of rural society, who then divert substantial quantities away from productive agricultural investments, if not out of the rural areas entirely. For example, it has been estimated that only 5 per cent of farmers in Africa and 15 per cent of farmers in Asia have access to formal credit; it is said in general of subsidized credit that 5 per cent of the farmers get 80 per cent of the credit, and that between 20 and 50 per cent of the funds lent usually find their way out of agriculture (Braverman and Gausch, p. 1255).

Small-scale farmers buying appropriate technology require only small loans, increasing administrative overheads

There are several economic and institutional reasons why credit is biased away from the poor. Firstly the administration costs of credit institutions are high; even the best ones have administration costs of a quarter of the value of loans made. As the costs of making small loans are higher, there results a direct financial pressure on the lending agency to make few large loans rather than many small ones. The lender must also make some

29

attempt to assess the creditworthiness of its borrowers to ensure that sufficient loans are repaid to sustain the financial viability of the credit system. The costs of assessing this information are very high, and by far the simplest approach is to disburse loans on the basis of observable wealth.

Co-operative credit schemes are an attempt to counter these problems. In Bangladesh, the Grameen Bank has some 300,000 members (of which 75 per cent are women) and has a repayment rate of 98 per cent (Nowak, 1988, p. 23; Bangladesh Institute of Development Studies, 1986). The reasons for this success were judged by Nowak and Devèze (1987, quoted by Michailof, 1987) to be:

○ the project . . . started from the analysis of the real needs of the rural population . . .;

○ the progressive adjustment . . . of an approach towards credit policy that was quite different from the practices of conventional banking;

○ free decision-making by the members . . . The members of the basic groups selected each other providing a guarantee of transparency and solidarity;

○ the double-checking of transactions at every level.

The staff of official credit organizations can be prejudiced and corrupt

Additionally, monopoly non-profit institutions foster patronage and corruption, and it is the wealthier sections of society that are best able to cultivate and utilize this weakness. Indeed it is not necessarily the case that the risks of delinquency are greater from the poor. In Costa Rica, for example, delinquency was actually found to be less for agricultural loans than for non-agricultural loans, and lowest on loans made to small farmers (Adams and Vogel, 1986, p. 138). It is important that the distinction is made between the willingness and the ability to repay a loan. Larger farmers may view loans as part of their political patronage, and have no intention of making repayments. One of the major incentives of making prompt repayment is to establish a record as a good borrower, and thus earn the right to take out larger loans at some later date. Aside from the possibility of more draconian action against the politically weak small farmers in the event of a default, this desire for future subsidized loans may also have greater effect.

The types of loans available may not be suitable for buying new technologies

Rural loans also typically have short-term maturities. This is done to minimize the chances of defaults, e.g. in the event of sustained weather problems, and to insure against inflationary losses. As loans are usually made with fixed nominal interest rates, increases in inflation can essentially eliminate the income from a loan. However, short-term loans are often at odds with the income profile generated by new technologies, which may take several years to cover their initial capital costs.

Rural credit is essential, but only one aspect of rural development, which has many dimensions

Credit plays an essential role in the financing of new technology. As we have observed, it is only one link in the chain of economic transformation from traditional to modern agriculture. In addition to controlling economic parameters such as agricultural prices and rural credit rates, public investment can be provided for infrastructure such as roads, irrigation, and rural electrification, or for providing basic social services such as health care and education. Funds can also be spent to develop local institutions and management capabilities, or more radically to redistribute resources within the rural community. In the next sections the approaches to rural development adopted by aid agencies and national governments are discussed.

The evolution of development strategies

Over the last few decades several different approaches to rural development have been advocated and followed to various extents. In the period immediately after World War II, the concept of Community Development came into vogue, and rapidly became a major focus of development assistance by donor countries. The Community Development approach was to attempt to build grass-roots democratic institutions that could contribute to the well-being of rural people 'without revolutionary changes in the existing political and economic order' (Holdcroft, 1978, p. 14; see also Birgegard, 1988, p. 7).

The phenomenon of Community Development expanded rapidly in the 1950s, and by 1960 more than 60 countries in Asia, Africa and Latin America had implemented or were in the process of implementing such programes (Ruttan, 1984, p. 393). By the middle of the 1960s, however, Community Development was being de-emphasized by both development assistance agencies and national governments. Major donors had withdrawn their support and most programmes had been terminated or considerably reduced. Attempts to mobilize the rural population to self-help action in democratic and locally controlled organizations had in practice been replaced by bureaucratic top-down delivery programmes (Birgegard, 1988, p. 9). Local elites had reaped a disproportionate share of programme benefits, leaving poor groups alienated.

In the 1970s the approach of Integrated Rural Development was adopted

The 1970s saw the arrival of the concept of Integrated Rural Development, similar to Community Development in its ideological origin and methodological content (Birgegard, 198; Cohen, 1980; Crawford, 1981; Crener *et al.*, 1983). It was a response to the apparent ineffectiveness of many of the infrastructure-oriented projects of the 1960s, and drew on complex and often contradictory intellectual and ideological perspectives (Cohen, 1980). An essential feature was the emergence of a 'systems approach' to thinking about institutional design and programme implementation. There was a perception that rural development involved the interaction of a large number of inter-related activities which had to be systematically planned. Research in the social sciences also drew increasing attention to the multidimensional nature of rural problems (economic, social, technical, etc) and called for broader development approaches.

Integrated Rural Development became an increasingly important model for develoment assistance projects (Ayres, 1983). Interestingly, it was the donor agencies rather than developing country governments that were responsible for its promotion (Ruttan, 1984, p. 393). One of the earliest IRD projects to be initiated with donor support was the Comilla project in Bangladesh (pioneered by the Pakistan Academy for Rural Development in 1959; see Khan, 1979) which, owing to its success in the initial stages, had far-reaching influences on rural development planners at the time, and paved the way for other projects in other countries (Ruttan, 1984, p. 394).

Integrated Rural Development was seen to have problems

By the early 1980s there was again a change of direction by some development agencies with Integrated Rural Development strategies being questioned in many quarters. There was a sudden decline in the enthusiasm regarding these programmes. This was not so much a retreat on equity goals, but rather a growing realization on the part of policy makers that the programmes, particularly in Africa, were not solving one of the most fundamental of rural problems — that of achieving a reliable food surplus (Eicher and Baker, 1982, p. 62). This resulted from rigid and inadequate administration.

Projects must incorporate grass-roots organizations, that can evaluate and adapt programmes to local conditions

The reasons for the decline in emphasis on the new directions of the 1970s were similar to those that led to the decline of Community Development in the early 1960s: primarily a perception that top-down bureaucracies and inflexible management approaches were nullifying the attempts at development. Particularly problematic was the need to co-ordinate many different activities that were dependent on each other for success. A review of the literature on rural devleopment shows that the efficient delivery of management and administrative services to rural areas is greatly dependent upon effective organization at the community level. Rural communities operating through either the formal structure of local government or voluntary institutions must be able to interact effectively with the central institutions which have the responsibility for the delivery of services to local communities.

The success of some pilot rural development projects has been due to the relative intensity in the use of human resources devoted to organization, management, and technical assistance. However, when attempts were made to generalize a pilot project as the model for a national or regional development programme (as with the Comilla project), the intensity of the human resource input could not be sustained. Added to this, access to the higher decision-making levels of government and the administrative flexibility to tailor projects precisely to local conditions that are often available to directors of pilot projects (or that can be generated by a few dynamic individuals) may be sacrificed for administrative convenience when the projects are generalized to a larger scale, or because sufficient numbers of skilled people are not available. Highly centralized administration of national programmes makes it difficult to carry out the experiments with programme content and delivery methods that are essential if rural development programes are to meet the diverse needs of rural areas (see Ruttan, 1984, p. 398).

'The approach of rural development (the *blueprint* approach) which uses projects designed beforehand by the administrative class and into which the peasants are asked to enter, in which there is a deep opposition towards any kind of initiative and organization on the part of peasants themselves that are not induced nor controlled by the State, and which systematically calls for subsidy policies for agricultural inputs rather than fair pricing policies for agricultural products, are aspects of African agricultural policies perfectly coherent with interests which have nothing to do with the defence of those of the rural populations' (Giri, 1986, p. 160).

Rather than adopt 'blueprint' solutions, projects must develop institutional capabilities at the local level

These recent perceptions of the problems of using a centralized 'blueprint' for development have led to a change in thought on appropriate project organization, although the idea that a project should comprise a package of different activities remains to some degree. This concept is sumarized by the *Manual for Preparing and Appraising Project and Programme Dossiers of the Commission of the European Communities*:

'Quite clearly, multisectoral measures may be needed in order to attain a sectoral objective: e.g. the objective of food security may necessitate reforms in transportation policy . . . It should, however, be noted that

33

this approach differs from that of integrated development which, in a given geographical context, is aimed at the concurrent attainment of a number of different sub-objectives such as production, health and education, a very ambitious approach which is therefore difficult to implement. In the sectoral approach, the important thing is the critical path identifying the relationships between key factors in order to attain a specific sectoral objective (e.g. food security); in this context, attention will only be paid to other objectives or other sectors in so far as they are essential to the success of an operation (e.g. in an irrigation project, a health objective may be included in order to fight against bilharziosis, without which the operation may not be able to work)' (VII/527/79–rev.2; Introduction, p. 2).

Energy sector investments often fall on a 'critical path'

It is also now argued that effective implementation of projects requires the development of institutional capacity at the local level. Consequently, project organizations should be designed in such a way that it can utilize the existing experience in rural areas. Usually there will be no option but to start with existing institutions, often non-governmental (see Drabeck, 1987, for a discussion of non-governmental organizations). Furthermore, project management must take an experimental view of their programmes. In principle it is not possible to design every dimension of a project at the initial planning stage (as may be implied by cost-benefit analysis with its assumption of perfect information on costs, behavioural changes, and benefits). Projects must adapt to changing circumstances and knowledge, and undergo an *evolutionary* response to the environment. Effective monitoring and evaluation is as a consequence vital.

The private sector may have an important role

One response to the difficulties of sustaining and duplicating development projects has been to emphasize the role of the private sector in delivering the goods and services needed by the project (see USAID, 1985). In a review of the experience of the United States Agency for International Development (1987, p. ix), Kumar observes:

'Most of the integrated rural development projects created or expanded large public sector entities for distributing credit, providing agricultural inputs, procuring agricultural produce, and marketing. Unfortunately, such organizations were not able to discharge their responsibilities for a variety of reasons. Bureaucratic procedures restricted the creativity and initiative of the project staff, especially at the field level. There was over-staffing. Often they lacked adequate resources to perform their duties. And low salaries, inadequate benefits, and restricted opportunities for career advancement did not attract high calibre staff.'

Because of these characteristics it is argued that public sector agencies usually can only respond sluggishly to changing conditions. Furthermore, the vertical organizational structures of many governmental bodies makes co-ordination of activities among different agencies difficult. Whether project inputs should be provided by private entrepreneurs or by local private voluntary organizations remains a topic of debate and political belief; nonetheless, the consensus amongst most international agencies is that at least one of these organizations should be utilized if possible. Clearly the economic environment in rural areas will strongly influence the attractiveness of private entrepreneurial activity.

'[certain accusations] are justified . . . (as for example) when the market structure enables [the merchant] to occupy a position of monopoly (a trader being able to control supply as well as purchases over a whole region or micro-region). On the other hand, when this monopoly cannot prevail, and when competition can take place, all the surveys show that private trade can provide a flexibility and a capacity for initiative, and the costs of intervention are such that the service it can render is much more effective than the one provided by any kind of state controlled organization, even one that is perfectly run . . . To this end, competition should be stimulated and quickened. This implies special efforts concerning:

○ road infrastructure . . .;

○ information: the greater use of radio and TV;

○ village organization . . . local associations . . . groups of regional associations . . .'
(Michailof, 1987, p. 206).

Some organizations are moving back to single sector projects

Some aid agencies faced reduced budgets in the late 1980s. The concept of integrated and evolutionary projects, while agreed as one possible approach, is outside the administrative capabilities of project managers, and beyond the financial resources allocated to rural development for a given country. In this situation the focus of activities is shifting back toward single targeted interventions; e.g. a road, an irrigation project, electricity distribution cables and transformers.

Local institutions are important, but resistance to the creation of effective institutions is only to be expected

To conclude this section, it is worth noting that the development of rural areas will in the future continue to be characterized by unequal rates of development between rural and urban areas, between different rural areas, and between social groups. A major implication of this is that in countries where the distribution of political resources is strongly biased against rural people it will continue to be difficult to mobilize the management resources necessary to make rural development programmes effective. There will probably also be strong resistance to the evolution of local institutions that have the capacity to mobilize resources for the rural poor. To counter this, it is likely that effective rural development will require many small but efficient actions (see also Michailof, 1987, p. 259).

Traditional energy and rural development

The demand for energy in rural areas comes from a variety of sources. Indeed there is hardly an activity of life that does not require the consumption of energy if one uses a broad technical definition. Following this description a school of 'energy fundamentalism' in the late 1970s added up the total units of energy consumed in a particular society and thus pronounced on its overall energy efficiency (defined as the primary energy input per unit of output measured in energy terms).

This is neither a useful criterion for judging the suitability of a particular farming system, nor a meaningful starting point for the analysis of development project interventions, because it neglects the cost of energy and the value of energy in different uses. Instead one must identify a set of activities that have specific policy implications, and that can be analysed in the context of the cultural, political and economic realities of rural communities.

Woodfuel deserves special attention in this section as it is the major source of energy in rural areas and often has limited substitutes. Wood, along with other biomass fuels such as agricultural residues and cattle dung, is used for domestic purposes, mainly cooking but also water heating. Other competing consumers are the urban poor, who consume wood and charcoal trucked in from rural areas, and rural industries. This latter group contains any businesses that require heat, and includes brickmaking, textiles, bakeries, breweries, tea drying, and tobacco curing. The on-farm processing of crops and the drying of fish can also require heat, and can compete with the home for wood. Finally, wood also has a variety of non-fuel uses as timber and poles.

The woodfuel problem

Deforestation can have severe environmental implications

The woodfuel problem has received much publicity, starting with its description as 'the other energy crisis' in the crisis-laden days of the 1970s (see, for example, Eckholm, 1975). The diagnosis of much of the literature of this topic is one of catastrophic destruction of natural forests, with consequent environmental decay. Reduced tree cover exposes soil to the

36

natural elements of sun, wind and water, which combine to destroy its food-producing capacity. Erosion removes fertile topsoil, while on the hills reduced water retention leads to flash floods, and on the plains winds generate dust-bowls. Thus, it has been argued, the depletion of forests will lead to a natural disaster on a global scale, the first signs of which can already be seen (CEC, 1986, *Le Courrier*, No. 95).

Simple models of wood consumption show that cutting wood for fuel leads to deforestation

This analysis follows simply from the perception that wood is being cut faster than it can regrow in existing forests. As forest is destroyed to meet the wood demand above the sustainable level, tree stocks are reduced and the level of sustainable production falls yet more. Disaster becomes inevitable as forests completely disappear. This end result would occur even if demand remained static at current levels, but is hastened by increasing populations.

Many models of wood supply and demand are built on the assumption of approximately constant annual demand for wood, together with a sustainable annual wood production rate from a unit of land. With an initial estimate of tree stocks and an estimate of population growth, it is a simple matter to calculate the area of forest that will be standing for each year in the future as it dwindles exponentially to zero. The underlying premise that collection of wood for fuel is the cause of deforestation in this way can be found in many studies including Anderson (1986), Anderson and Fishwick (1984), and de Montalembert and Clement (1983).

The causes of deforestation are many and complex

Are these models a satisfactory representation of reality? Is the use of wood for fuel the major cause of deforestation? Is environmental catastrophe inevitable unless there is an unprecedented intervention by governments and aid agenices to dramatically increase the numbers of trees growing in developing countries? As with most questions of this type there are few simple answers. However, it is probably true that although there are localized areas of severe deforestation, where one can literally go for miles without seeing trees, some aspects of the woodfuel problem (as distinct from the forest problem) have been exaggerated in the past.

As with all simple system dynamic models of the kind described above, proper account is not taken of a variety of behavioural changes that occur when a commodity becomes more scarce and therefore more costly. In one way or another people will use less wood as it becomes harder to get. Equally, the increased value of wood can lead to a supply response with wood being grown by private individuals. These combined effects much reduce the depletion of forest from fuel consumption that would otherwise be predicted.

The prospect of environmental disaster does exist. Statistics show large-scale deforestation in many areas; in Africa, for example, the loss of forest and savannah woodland is put at 3.6 million hectares per year (Spares, 1986; quoted by Leach and Mearns, 1988, p. 1). Some of the most pressing areas for concern are in the Sahel, where drought combined with abuse of the environment from over-grazing and deforestation are leading to irrecoverable desertification (see Falloux and Makendi, 1988 and World Bank, 1985a; Bonfils, 1987).

However, the emphasis on such major questions outside of a few critical locations diverts from many more immediate issues. An emphasis on increasing the numbers of trees, for instance, may lead one to propose large-scale re-forestry programmes, when these may do little to help the people who are suffering from the increased scarcity of wood. To assess the appropriateness of policies to counter wood scarcity one must first consider in more detail the mechanisms that lead to deforestation.

The spread of agriculture may be the major cause of deforestation

There are various consumers of wood, and the role of each group must be considered carefully. The loss of forest may be resulting from factors unrelated to the collection of wood for domestic cooking. Indeed, in the view of many, population pressure does lead to deforestation, but not because of the direct cutting of wood for fuel. Instead population growth leads to pressures for more farmland, and natural woodlands are cleared to grow food. Spears (1986; quoted by Leach and Mearns, 1988, p. 12) estimates that some two-thirds of permanent forest loss in Africa between 1950 and 1983 was due to land clearance. Because of this situation it is possible for there to be wood surpluses while extensive deforestation is going on (e.g. in Sri Lanka). This may hide the fact that severe wood shortages and environmental stress are imminent.

The use of woody biomass in households

In some countries wood may account for up to 90 per cent of all energy consumption

Wood is the preferred fuel for families that cannot afford charcoal, coal or kerosene and the relevant stove. Indeed in many countries wood is a major source of energy even at a national level. The percentage of total primary demand coming from wood for some African countries is shown in Table 1. Wood makes a more important relative contribution as a fuel in African countries than elsewhere, due to the level and structure of their industries.

The consumption of wood is very location specific

Household consumption varies by location. In some areas annual wood consumption can be very high, reportedly as high as 2,865 kg per head in Nicaragua and 2,600 kg per head in Tanzania (Foley, 1985, p. 225). Usually consumption estimates are much less than this; however, data samples are often very small and there is conflicting evidence from different studies. As Foley (1988a, p. 2) notes, the measured consumption per head in different village surveys within both Burkina Faso and Nicaragua has differed by a factor of two to three. This is also true of some surveys in the Pacific Islands (PEDP, 1986, p. 6–12) even when carried out under the same supervisors.

With this proviso, a per capita consumption of between 0.5 cubic metres and 1.0 cubic metres is typical for many areas (see de Montalembert and Clement, 1983). For an average conversion factor assume that one cubic metre of stacked wood, air-dried and ready for use, weighs approximately 400 kg. Its heating value would be of the order of 15 MJ/kg, half that of anthracite, and one-third that of kerosene.

Table 1   The percentage fuel mix in meeting total energy demand

Country	Year	Fuelwood	Charcoal	Other biomass fuels	Petroleum	Other commercial fuels
Low income						
Somalia	1984	77	5	5	12	1
Niger	1980	86	—	—	12	2
Ethiopia	1982	37	1	55	7	1
Tanzania	1981	88	4	—	7	1
Ghana	1985	59	10	5	23	3
Malawi	1980	91	—	3	4	2
Uganda	1982	90	4	—	6	1
Kenya	1985	65	9	—	24	1
Middle income						
Liberia	1983	61	8	—	23	9
Zambia	1981	25	6	1	18	52
Ivory Coast	1982	52	4	9	31	5
Zimbabwe	1980	25	—	3	11	61
Congo	1985	45	1	1	49	5

Source: UNDP/World Bank Energy Assessment Reports; quoted by World Bank, 1987a, table 1.2.

Note: Calculating primary energy consumption is a notably difficult task, with a large degree of unreliability in the results. Consequently, this data should only be viewed as indicative in nature.

Wood comes from many sources, not just felling trees in forests

Fuelwood comes from fallen and dead branches and twigs, as a by-product from other wood products (e.g. poles and timber), from tree cutting for fuel, and from felling to clear agricultural land. Trees grow on private land, on hedgerows and along paths, and on communal or government land. The proportion of wood coming from each source depends upon location, the size of a household's land-holdings, and its social status.

Wood on common land is often mismanaged when woodfuel resources become scarce

Wood growing on communal land is a *free* resource for wood gatherers in the sense that they neither pay cash for it nor invest in its cultivation. As with all *common resources* (including fisheries in Europe) there is an incentive for an individual to collect as much as is needed without heed to the effect it will have on other people collecting from the same area. Wood therefore has a classic attribute of a *public good*; its social cost is above its private collection cost to the individual (see Dorfman and Dorfman, 1977). Two key issues result from this: first, when resources become scarce there may be environmental mismanagement and excessive wood harvesting. This is the 'tragedy of the commons', as it was named by Hardin (1986). Second, as fuelwood has no financial cost to the user, it is preferred by poor people to all other energy options which require cash expenditures. This key point is discussed in more detail later in this chapter.

However, it must be noted that the problems of overcropping of wood is as much associated with the breakdown of traditional management systems as with overpopulation *per se*. Many communities have succeeded in controlling their forestry resources by restricting access by people outside the community (see Repetto and Holmes, 1983). As these restrictions break down, wood resources shift from being *common* to the community, to *free access* for all. Even with some degree of co-operative action and community control, there can still be the problem of *free-riders* who collect more than they should if the system were to benefit the whole community.

Wood also comes from the private land of the collectors and that of other households

In areas where agriculture has spread to cover most of the land, such as in large parts of South Asia, woodfuel comes mainly from trees owned by private individuals rather than 'forests' (see Leach, 1987). The fuel status of a household is then a direct reflection of its access to private land. Poor households not owning land may still be allowed on the land of others if there exists traditional patron–client relationships with wealthier households, often their employers (see Howes, 1985).

The access to the land of others changes as wood becomes scarce

As the pressures from population increase on the remaining tree resources, these traditional relationships break down. First, the poor will be prevented from taking preferred types of wood. If wood scarcity worsens they will at some stage be excluded from taking any kind of wood. The poor will then have to use agricultural residues (e.g. maize stalks) and dried cattle dung collected from the fields of others for fuel. This is true for much of India, for example. Eventually, even these resources will be restricted to them, and they will have to collect unwanted leaves, and steal better fuels when they have the opportunity. An example of this transition in social relationships was observed by Briscoe (1979) in his study of a Bangladeshi village. Unfortunately this dynamic description of how the rural fuel situation changes over time is normally not available to policy makers, who must make decisions on the basis of static 'snapshot' surveys of fuel demand and supply.

The choice between wood and agricultural residues is complex, often determined more by the poverty of specific groups than by overall shortages

These transitions certainly cause a greater deterioration in the welfare of the landless poor than that of landowners. It is important to recognize that alternative biomass fuels do exist, however, some of which may be almost as suitable as wood (dung mixed with certain residues is slow burning and is used to parboil rice even in areas where wood is available). As wood scarcity increases it is natural that people should shift to these fuels. The trade-offs are sophisticated and wood may have to be cheap to be competitive. Thus, the poorer sections of rural society may not wish to consume wood if they had to pay the full social cost of using it.

This is a reflection of poverty and low purchasing power. It is not a desirable state, and it may imply considerable hardship for some members of the rural community, particularly poor women. The key point is that interventions to address woodfuel scarcities must account for the fact that many poor people may only be able to afford wood if it is available free except for their collecting time. This is the very condition that led to environmental mismanagement in the first place. Later in this chapter we discuss the appropriateness of forestry and stove projects because of these inequalities.

Burning agricultural residues may reduce food production

Since the burning of agricultural residues can remove green fertilizers from fields, it is possible for the nitrogen content of soils to fall. In this event agricultural production would fall, perhaps in a cumulative fashion as soils became progressively degraded. However, not all biomass resources are suitable as fertilizer. Cotton stalks, for example, are too woody, and maize stalks left in the fields can harbour pests. The extent to which the use of biomass as fuel will cause a deterioration in crop yields will vary dramatically from farming system to farming system and from region to region. When it occurs it will often be associated with other environmental stress resulting from over-cropping and over-grazing.

41

Residues can be replaced with commercial fertilizers, and in some cases this may be optimal for farmers

Consider the case of a family growing 2 hectares of grain on the same plot each year. Their land may yield 2 tonnes of grain with some irrigation and fertilizer. This should produce approximately 4 tonnes of residue. If this provided for half the energy consumption of the household, perhaps a quarter (i.e. 1 tonne) of the agricultural residue would be burnt. At a nitrogen content of 1 per cent (FAO, 1979), this biomas would remove 10 kg of nitrogen from the fields. Assuming a 20:1 ratio of additional crop output to added nitrogen (i.e. an 8:1 ratio of additional crop to an added commercial fertilizer such as urea; World Bank, 1979), the yield of the following year's harvest could potentially be reduced by 200 kg, a 10 per cent fall. However, additional commercial nitrogen fertilizer could be added. Using the above crude estimates, one tonne of residue could be replaced by 10 kg of nitrogen. If this nitrogen cost $0.9 per kg (e.g. delivered urea at $330 per tonne) the price of fuel to the household would be $9, equivalent to a substitute wood price of $14 per tonne. The value of wood varies from location to location, but will often not fall this low. This result is similar to the conclusion by Newcombe (1984, p. 15), in a case study in Ethiopia, that:

> '. . . sound logic is applied by farmers in selling their [cattle] dung to urban markets as a source of cash. In the present market place, dung returns more when sold as a fuel than can be obtained, on average, in the form of additional grain production through its use as fertilizer'.

It is open to question when the drain on the fertility of soil from the burning of residues is cause for concern (Devron, Egg and Lerin, 1979). *The issue to be remembered is that if agricultural projects do not take fuel use into account, yields may be less than planned. Similarly, a loss of groundcover will increase soil erosion and the siltation of canals and dams. The life of irrigation and hydro-power projects may be shorter than expected for the rural fuel market is not understood and energy demands catered for.*

Wood, women and health

Women are responsible for cooking and often responsible for collecting fuel

An increase in the scarcity (or cost) of wood, even if it does not indicate environmental catastrophe, must be borne by the rural community. These costs are not spread equally across all members. Although there are variations both within and between societies with regard to the work that women do, there is a well-established tendency for women to be responsible for the domestic processing and preparation of food. Along with this goes an almost exclusive responsibility for the fuel-using activities of cooking, and the heating of water for washing. The responsibility of women also tend to extend into the area of fuel collection for cooking, although men sometimes perform the heavier cutting and transporting tasks and are responsible for securing specific types of fuel.

As a consequence of the unequal distribution of its costs, the scarcity of fuelwood and the increasing use of poor quality fuels may be taking a considerable toll on certain aspects of family welfare. Clearly, women are the most seriously affected since they are the ones who have to walk longer distances in search of fuelwood or to look for alternative fuels for their family's needs. Women can spend hours each day gathering fuel and have to walk for several kilometres (see Agarwal, 1986; Cecelski, 1987; ILO, 1986a).

Increased wood scarcity can have health effects if cooking practices and diets change

One significant impact of increased wood scarcity may be that fewer meals are cooked, possibly with adverse effects on those who eat the meals. Meals cooked early in the morning, but not eaten until late in the evening, are not as fresh and could even become contaminated. In cooler regions the effects of going without a hot meal, hot water, and heat from a fire are more serious, particularly for the sick and elderly.

Diets also change as a response to fuel shortages. In Sri Lanka, for example, where rice is the staple food, many poor landless families are gradually replacing at least one of their rice meals with bread. In this case the bread is made from white flour with a lower nutritional content than the traditional rice dish. In the central highlands of Mexico women cite a lack of large logs of slow-burning timber as the reason that they are now cooking fewer beans, the principle source of protein for the poor (Cecelski, 1985, p. 38).

Burning residues produces more smoke and may cause health problems

The burning of substitutes for wood, such as crop and animal residues, green twigs etc, also produces more smoke. In poorly ventilated kitchens the amount of smoke inhaled by women and children increases. Seminal work by Smith *et al.* (1983) has indicated that the levels of smoke in kitchens are a serious health problem, leading to respiratory and heart disease. In measurements in kitchens in Gujarati villages, the estimated annual dose of women cooking is 5,800 mg of Total Suspended Particles (TSP) and 3,200 mg of Benzopyrene. The TSP pollutant level is more than 100 times the level found with indoor wood heating in the US; the Benzopyrene figure is *equivalent to smoking 20 packets of cigarettes per day!* (Smith *et al.*, 1983, tables 8 and 9).

Woodfuel problems can also prevent women earning income from food processing

Women are often involved with food processing in addition to the needs of their own families, such as brewing, baking, and the smoking of fish. This produce is sold to neighbours or traders, and gives one of the few opportunities for women to earn cash. Cooking meals is the first priority, so that an increase in fuel scarcity can very rapidly make this cottage food production difficult. The control of some cash allows women to purchase independently some items that may not otherwise enter into the family budget. This could include kitchen appliances that would increase the productivity of their cooking time. Clearly, the loss of such income may have major implications for the welfare of women.

The woodfuel crisis is often the poor women's crisis

It is obvious that spending more time collecting fuel reduces the time that women have for looking after their families and training their children. If children also help to collect wood, then they do not only lose the attention of their parents, but also have less time for education. For some families, then, the negative effects of fuelwood scarcity are pervasive, and affect all productive functions of women in the household. One dimension of programmes designed to improve the status of women should be to consider methods of reducing the time spent collecting fuel and cooking.

The participation of men in the rural wood market indicates that the sexual division of labour in fuel collection is much less sex-typed as women's work than for example water fetching or cooking. Also the increased distances that must be walked to collect fuel appear to be encouraging some flexibility towards the roles of men and women. The most important factor is whether some of the changes which are occurring in wood markets in some areas will improve household fuel supply and relieve women's work burden, or simply remove their access to preferred cooking fuels. This latter course is more likely to be the case for poor households with limited land ownership. To paraphrase Howes (1985, p. 80), the rural fuelwood crisis is really the poor women's crisis.

Competing demands for wood

Urban markets can be major consumers of wood

While most fuelwood remains outside the market economy, a growing proportion is traded for money. The commercialization of wood markets, usually to supply urban consumers in the first instance, leads to a direct drain on the wood available to rural people. The World Bank (1987a, table 3.1) estimates the proportion of woodfuel taken by urban areas in the following countries to be:

Ivory Coast (1982)	22 per cent
Liberia (1983)	15 per cent
Zimbabwe (1980)	16 per cent
Zambia (1981)	9 per cent
Ethiopia (1982)	10 per cent
Uganda (1982)	2 per cent
Kenya (1985)	11 per cent
Burundi (1980)	10 per cent
Niger (1980)	20 per cent

City populations are also growing rapidly in many places, and the urban demand for wood can be expected to burgeon in the future. The urban population of Africa will double in the next ten years, while rural areas will grow by only 20 per cent. Thus the urban poor will become an ever more important customer for rural wood.

Wood is taken long distances to urban areas

Wood can be trucked hundreds of kilometres to cities. The price paid for wood in rural areas is negotiated with the collectors who carry it to road-sides. The *opportunity cost* of underemployed people can be very little (their output in the next best alternative activity), so the price of wood can be very low. There are quality constraints on the types of wood that can be taken to cities due to size and smokiness, and bushes and smaller trees are left behind. This means that although the stock of large trees can be devastated (often illegally) by truckers, they move on to new areas before complete deforestation including small trees takes place.

As distances increase the additional transportation costs give incentives for people to grow wood nearer the city. Table 2 presents some estimates of the cost of trucking wood. Going from a 50 km trip to one of 100 km adds another $9 per tonne of wood to costs. As transportation distances increase above 100 km, wood production near the city may become economic, depending upon growing costs.

Charcoal is brought even further

However, the economics of wood production change if charcoal is transported to cities. Charcoal is predominantly an urban fuel, where it is preferred to wood for its ease of use and lack of smoke. It has twice the energy content per unit weight, but is often four times the cost of wood by weight (depending upon moisture content, and the particular fuels considered). Some five to eight tonnes of wood are used to make one tonne of charcoal. Therefore, an increase in transport costs of $9 per tonne coming from an increase in distance from 50 km to 100 km is transformed into an increase in the cost of wood nearer to the city of only $1.5 per tonne. In a charcoal market, fuel can be brought from hundreds of kilometres before wood could be grown and charcoal made more cheaply adjacent to the city.

Table 2   Transportation costs of wood and charcoal

Distance (km)	Fuelwood transportation costs, $/tonne	Charcoal transportation costs, $/tonne
25	15.3	14.6
50	21.6	20.6
100	30.5	29.1
200	43.2	41.1
500	65.0	68.3

Source: Analysis of wood transport with 7-tonne trucks in Kenya; World Bank, 1987a, table 1.4.

The marketing chain of wood and charcoal is complex

However, the wood and charcoal transportation system is complex, and the above analysis may be too simple. For example, large margins often exist between the price of wood in cities and that in rural reas. To quote Leach (1987, p. 69):

'In Malawi there is an estimated 15-fold difference between the sale price for rural producers and the final market price . . . In Nicaragua the equivalent figure for sales in Managua is a factor of 12.'

The marketing chain from the up-country roadside to kitchen stove can include rural fuelwood contractors, the transporters, urban wholesalers, and retailers. Each of these stages can have large mark-ups. In a study of charcoal transportation in Kenya, the World Bank (1987a, p. 38) estimated that transporters were paid 2.5 times their costs for taking charcoal to Nairobi. The structure of retail charcoal costs was estimated (ibid, table 2.6) to be:

Roadside costs	29 per cent
Transportation cost	15 per cent
Transporters' profit margin	20 per cent
Wholesalers' gross margin	13 per cent
Retailers' margin for lost material	10 per cent
Retailers' remaining gross margin	18 per cent

Similar large mark-ups have been measured with woodfuels in Hyderabad, India (Alam and Dunkerly, 1983) and in Bangladesh (Prior, 1984). However, while wood may be sold at several times its cost, the volumes sold by petty traders may be such that wood truckers do not earn more than other truckers, or the minimum urban wage.

The effect of taxes on cutting wood are not obvious

It has been suggested that the introduction of *stumpage taxes*, i.e. a tax taking wood into cities, would help raise the price of wood to its social cost. This can have three effects: to increase the price in the city; to reduce truckers', retailers' and wholesalers' margins; or to reduce the price offered to collectors to a minimum, if it is not there already. While taxes will generate revenue, they will only reduce wood consumption if the first two of these responses takes place. If they reduce the price paid to producers, then the growing of wood becomes less attractive. Revenue collection has its cost, and may also present some complications.

Urban demand management may be the most effective method of increasing wood supplies to rural people

The urban wood market exists alongside the rural market and there are complex linkages between the two. Interventions in the rural market may be nullified if these interactions are not properly understood. Conversely, programmes of demand management in urban areas may pay dividends on the rural fuelwood situation. Urban wood burners have the feature of being concentrated in a few locations, making programme organization easier. Even though there may be detrimental impacts on poor women, the sale of wood to cities does allow the rural poor male to earn some cash income. In this situation the poor family may choose to burn inferior biomass if it means cash in their pockets.

Rural industries also use wood, sometimes large amounts locally, but typically little at a national level

One of the important dimensions of rural development is the growth of rural industries. Some of these process agricultural produce so that it can be better transported to market centres. This helps to stimulate demand for agricultural products, and keeps a larger proportion of value-added in rural areas. For items such as bricks and tiles, local manufacture is the only feasible way for these goods to reach rural people. All such industries require energy, and those that need heat to dry and cure produce (e.g. tobacco curing, tea drying, and fish smoking), or to fire clay (e.g. bricks and pottery) use large quantities of wood. These organizations add to the number of consumer groups using wood, and add yet more complication to the rural wood market.

The fact that individual industries burn large quantities of wood is often swamped in national statistics because there are relatively few of them. For example, the wood consumption in Tanzania has been estimated at 1.3 million cubic metres for tobacco curing, and approximately 0.6 million cubic metres for pottery, brickmaking, fish smoking and tea drying. This

47

compares with wood consumption in the entire country of between 20 and 30 million cubic metres. Rural cottage industries in Kenya have been estimated to use 2.7 million cubic metres of wood, of a national wood consumption of 19 million cubic metres (FAO internal reports).

Rural industries come in all forms and sizes, from self-employed individuals, families and groups of families to larger organizations with employed work-forces, and wood use varied dramatically. A small brickmaker producing one thousand bricks per day can burn more than one thousand tonnes of wood per year, perhaps the same amount as an entire village.

Moving all industries towards best practice techniques can save large quantities of wood at a local level

The efficiency with which wood is consumed for these and other activities are often well below that achievable from best practice techniques. The availability of wood can be essential for the success of these industries, although they usually contribute no more than a few per cent to national wood consumption. Interventions to improve fuel use would do well to consider a group of industries in order to have maximum impact.

Charcoal production uses wood, usually wood that is free

Charcoal making is a little different from other rural industries as wood is used as a combined feedstock and heat source. Charcoal is also sold as an alternative fuel to wood, so that its production has a direct effect on wood demand. This means that if charcoal were not made, wood consumption need not necessarily fall. However, charcoal consumption is predominantly an urban phenomenon, so that it still represents a loss of wood to the rural community. Furthermore, charcoal is often made in locations where transporting raw wood to town would be uneconomic. In some areas of Africa it is a major source of cash for subsistence farmers.

Charcoal is made from the partial combustion of wood. With traditional methods a pile of wood is covered with earth to restrict the access of air. The wood is lit and allowed to smoulder to produce charcoal. Efficiencies with this process are low, normally about 15 to 20 per cent by weight, or some 30 to 40 per cent in terms of energy. In fact the term *charcoal* is somewhat ambiguous. It is a combination of carbon, tars, and partially pyrolysed wood. The efficiency of charcoal manufacture depends upon the quality of the product, with more energy needed to produce purer carbon. Even so, for a given quality the traditional production techniques require more wood than more sophisticated technologies.

In most developing countries, charcoal is made from wood that is collected from the clearing of natural forests and woodlands. It is free to the charcoal maker except for the costs of the labour involved. As charcoal has more energy per unit weight than wood, it can be economically transported

48

long distances from areas where there is wood to urban markets: in Sudan and Senegal it is reported that charcoal is trucked up to 500 km (World Bank, 1987, p. 36).

New charcoal-making technologies are unlikely to be adopted unless the access to wood is regulated

Numerous new designs of charcoal kiln have been suggested (see ILO 1975; Little, 1975; Tropical Products Institute, 1980; and VITA, 1980). They are usually of a transportable steel design. However, if the price of wood is low, as it usually is, there is little incentive to invest in either more sophisticated and expensive brick-built beehive kilns or these improved metal designs. The new designs increase the efficiency of conversion, but they may reduce the profits of the operator.

Unless the access to wood is restricted, programmes to introduce new kilns will probably fail. However, new technolgoies can be introduced if access is allowed to hitherto restricted land owned by the forestry department. Charcoal makers can be used for part of the normal process of tree thinning. Permission to use this wood can be conditional on the use of certain types of kiln. Charcoal makers on forestry department land, competing with more remote producers, may be induced to invest in equipment. The forestry department can also cover some of the initial capital expenditure. The use of the Mark V metal kiln in Uganda in the 1960s was part of a project of this kind, where controlled admission to forestry department land was an important component of the overall programme (Foley, 1988a).

Policy interventions for woodfuel

In recent years both governments and international aid agenices have become aware of the deforestation that is taking place in many regions. A range of different initiatives have been taken both to increase the supply and to reduce the demand for wood. On the supply side there are programmes to plant trees either in large-scale forestry projects, or through social forestry, which involves local people planting their own trees. Demand-side measures feature the introduction of new types of stoves which are supposed to be more efficient in their use of fuel than traditional hearths and stoves (Madon and Matley, 1986).

Forestry programmes to increase wood supply

In many countries the planting of trees is regarded as a major solution to deforestation. In the 1950s and 1960s the focus in most countries was on industrial forestry projects, with complementary sawmills and pulp and paper plants. In these cases either private corporations or the state forestry department develop large-scale plantations. The required management activities of the foresters include the planting of selected tree species, and the usual silviculture activities of thinning and the removal of undesirable tree types. The same approach can be followed when forests are planted for environmental and development reasons, in this case by the forestry department on government land. When wood is in short supply, normally a precondition for environmental concerns, the forestry department staff must also regulate access to the forest and the unauthorized cutting of wood (see World Bank, 1978; Grut, 1986).

Assessing the economics of forestry projects is particularly difficult because of the long periods required for trees to grow to maturity and the nature of the benefits involved. Trees provide the direct benefits of fuelwood, forage, and construction timber. Attempts can be made to assess the value of these commodities; for example, fuelwood from the forest may substitute for animal dung as a domestic fuel. The fertilizer value of dung can be estimated, and a rough measure of the gain in crop production from unburnt dung can be calculated (see Newcombe, 1984, for a case study in Ethopia; and Anderson, 1987, for a case study in northern Nigeria). More nebulous are the environmental benefits from tree cover such as the reduction of soil erosion from wind and water. These are major long-term benefits that take decades to be realized. If they can be quantified, environmental benefits have little present value in the normal procedures of cost-benefit analysis, which takes into account the cost of tying up resources and capital with a non-zero social discount or interest rate.

Social forestry

Although the resources needed for projects run by the state forestry department can be to some degree autonomous of the local community (with some hiring of labour), the involvement of local people is nonetheless crucial. The manpower available to the forestry department to police its land is limited. In areas of wood shortages it is only to be expected that people will come to the plantations and cut wood for their own needs and to sell to others. In general this theft of wood is likely to thwart the managed harvesting of trees. This is indeed a major problem for centrally organized forestry projects in regions where tree stocks are depleted, and tree planting will only succeed if local people have some involvement in the management of the forest. Because of this and the apparent exclusion of the poor from the benefits of large-scale industrial forestry projects, the emphasis moved in the 1980s to social or agro-forestry projects. These are also methods of reducing the costs of establishing trees by getting the recipient population to bear some of the costs.

The relatively recent approach of social forestry is social in the sense that its goal is to induce local people to plant their own trees. This may involve community organizations planting trees on common land, or individual farmers growing trees on private holdings.

The role of the project sponsors varies in different cases. Often a sympathetic organization provides seedlings and information on appropriate silviculture techniques although farmers can also provide their own seedlings, or use cuttings. The forestry department may also supply assistance with land clearance if new species are to be grown. Large sums of money have been spent on social forestry projects. For example, the World Bank in the last decade has devoted 60 per cent of its forestry budget to supporting smallholder tree growing (Leach and Mearns, 1988, p. 61). Other international agencies have made a similar shift. The United States Agency for International Development has on-going projects in Bangladesh, India, and Nepal with a total budget of more than $150 million. In one of these projects, the Madhya Pradesh Social Forestry Project, over 13 million tree seedlings were distributed to farmers free of charge in 1985 (MacKie, 1986). In Haiti another programme of USAID distributed 27 million seedlings to 110,000 farmers over the first five years of the programme (USAID, 1984; quoted by Leach and Mearns, 1988, p. 108).

Many village woodlots have had difficulties, because of complexities over the control of land

Organizing the successful and sustained growing of trees by local people is far from an easy task. In many locations village woodlots have failed to give expected results. The main problems are the complex social regulations regarding ownership of land, access to it, and the rights to any trees growing on it. Land officially designated as being communal or government land may in fact have been appropriated by individual households. In a case study of social forestry in Azad Kashmir, Pakistan (1985, p. 275), Cernea describes the takeover of shamilat community land:

'Village families whose land adjoined the shamilat areas began to divide the shamilat among themselves and numerous small and remote farmers were left out of this informal partitioning. . . . These village families began to take over the land and even to cultivate it. Rights to shamilat land became transferable through inheritance or sale of fractions of the privately owned areas, which carry with them rights to proportionate fractions of shamilat lots. While this appropriation advanced, shamilat kept is formal status as community land and was not entered in the revenue records as belonging to private families. As a result, the families concerned did not have to pay land taxes on 'their' shamilat plots'.

In this situation, attempts to establish trees on community land are unlikely to have the planned effect. Either farmers operating the community land will prefer to use the land for other activities and refuse to co-operate, or they will assume that they have ownership rights over the trees grown there. This will have adverse effects if poor households were previously permitted to graze their animals on communal land but are now prohibited from doing so.

Mismanagement is likely unless existing local councils are included, but this has implications for the distribution of benefits

Even if truly communal land exists and trees are planted, unsustainable cutting of wood may well occur for the very same reasons that natural woodland became deforested in the first place. The problem of common woodland will not be eliminated unless the local community creates and enforces appropriate rules controlling the cutting of wood. This has led to the conclusion that the organization of village woodland must incorporate existing structures of authority within rural areas (see Wade, 1987). Complex regulations already exist for many facets of rural life, it is argued. Moreover, in many cases these regulations directly address social costs not taken into account in the unrestricted market. Examples include the management of irrigation from communal sources and the management of grazing. Clearly similar institutions for managing woodland can be conceptualized. Indeed there are often already codes in force regarding access to wood, although they may require adaptation and stronger enforcement.

The problem remains that power in villages is concentrated in the hands of a few families. The local woodland police will be under the influence of these local elites, with obvious implications for the distribution of the benefits of an enhanced wood supply. Wade (1987) argues that local councils need not be unequitable, and that examples exist in South India of fair local organizations. An important factor, he argues, is that the council addresses only those factors that have non-privatizable benefits, thus reducing potential conflicts.

These propositions may be plausible when one is considering the distribution of free goods (such as water and forage), but are less likely to hold when resources must be put into production (particularly land in the case of tree planting) and when the product has a cash value or has a very high opportunity cost. This is the typical situation when community woodland is considered. It follows that programmes of community forestry must be preceded by a thorough understanding of the social hierarchy in the areas where trees are to be grown. Local participation is obviously needed, but it must also be recognized that the effectiveness of this participation will depend upon the extent to which a project interacts with the existing conflicts in the community.

The private growing of trees eliminates some of the problems found with community projects because rights of access to trees are better defined

If farmers grow their own trees on their own land many of these problems are reduced, although some may still remain. Landowners for instance may contest the rights to the trees which sharecroppers plant, as may farmers planting hedgerow along paths. The basic criterion for most farmers is the unequivocal right to do what they will with the trees that they plant. A more disaggregated categorization would include rights to plant trees, rights to cut wood including complete felling, rights to exclude others from taking wood, and rights to inherit. Nonetheless, the prospects for success of farm-based forestry schemes are greater than community schemes, because ownership rights are better defined, either *de jure* or *de facto*.

Integrating woodfuel projects with other projects that require wood products can increase tree planting

Growing trees until they reach a level of maturity when they can be harvested for fuelwood may take some years, although fast-growing species and coppicing may reduce this delay. The additional reward from tree cultivation is that the tree will have a cash value, and can be cut down at times when money is needed (see Chambers and Leach, 1987). Only the richer farmers who have surplus time to generate savings will be prepared to put effort into planting trees and protecting them from animals and thieves. The more pressing problems of maximizing agricultural production from the next harvest are understandably foremost in the mind of most farmers.

Incorporating woodland projects into other types of project is one way of trying to overcome the hurdle of no short-term returns. An important example of this is the use of tree species that provide fodder from leaves, pods and young twigs. In Kenya, for example, a dairy development project has experimented with fodder trees to provide much needed protein and roughage. The seedlings and silviculture advice are provided from a nearby woodfuel programme (Leach and Mearns, 1988, example 3.2).

In the final analysis people will grow trees if it is in their interest to do so. Supplying seedlings is far from a sufficient inducement. New forestry technologies cannot alone provide the solution to re-forestation. For example, rapidly growing tree species, most particularly *Leucaena lucocephala* (or *Ipil-ipil*), have been widely diffused around the world to areas where it was previously unknown. A new insect pest has also followed the *Leucaena* (possibly carried by foreign forestry experts), and large-scale defoliation has already occurred in the Philippines and Indonesia. Concern has also been expressed over eucalyptus plantations. While still controversial, it is argued that in some cases these plantations compete with crops or groundcover for water; are ineffective at controlling soil erosion; and significantly reduce the diversity of wildlife (Mackie, 1986, p. 33). Reliance on a single species can be a high-risk strategy if it should turn out to be an inappropriate choice.

More important to farmers is the possibility of being able to obtain some direct economic benefit from the trees they grow. Thus in Asia the commercial channels for selling wood are such that tree planting can be a profitable agricultural activity. This is unlikely to be true for much of Africa. Combining fuelwood projects with other projects to increase the return from growing trees is one method of spreading incentives to other areas. These could be new woodburning rural industries, or agricultural development projects that require fodder, poles, and fruit.

Stove programmes to decrease wood consumption

Rural populations have responded to woodfuel problems by using alternative sources of fuel. Under the pressure of scarcity, they economize on wood, and change their cooking utensils, their way of cooking, and sometimes even their cooking stoves. Traditionally, cooking is done on simple mud stoves or open fires (e.g. the *three-stone* fire). Although the technical efficiency of these methods depends upon the skill of the operator, and quite high efficiencies have been measured both in laboratories and in the field (see Visser and Verhaart, 1980; Gill, 1983a), there is a consensus that the quantity of fuel burnt in the typical home could be reduced if new stove designs were adopted. Many calculations assume an efficiency of traditional stoves of between 5 and 10 per cent, which if doubled at a national level would free vast quantities of wood. Although there is debate over the exact costs and benefits of new stoves, there has been a general agreement in many agencies that they would constitute one of the most promising, and rapid, solutions to the woodfuel crisis.

A large number of stove projects have had problems as a result of a misjudgement of needs

While there have been some notable successes as a result of initiatives to diffuse new stoves, particularly in China, a large number of programmes elsewhere have failed to win the support of the people they were meant to help. There have been some technical mistakes in design, but above all the external perception of the problem, whatever its apparent logic and validity, fails to convince potential consumers (see Islam *et al.*, 1984, p. 10). It has often been the case that once the visiting experts and extension workers leave, the carefully constructed energy-saving stoves, even if they are used until they are worn out, are not replaced (see Bialy, 1986; Foley and Moss, 1983; Manibog, 1984).

Studies of earlier stove projects raised doubts about the technical feasibility of the proposed stoves, about the way in which they would fit into the working patterns of the kitchen, and whether they could be introduced on a regional or national scale. Part of the problem with the first programmes was that they focused on the fuel efficiency of the stoves without actually considering how they would be used in the kitchen. However, stove designers are now becoming aware of the many different functions of the cooking fire.

It is now generally known, for example, that rural women will certainly be more attracted to a new stove if it offers a combination of benefits. Saving woodfuel is not their only priority; they desire stoves which allow speedy cooking, are easy to use, are safer, and produce less smoke (Gill, 1987). This does not mean that saving fuel is unimportant in the choice of stove, just that it is but one aspect of a complex problem. The acceptability of a stove also depends upon its cost and ease of installation. The price of the stove, or the materials needed for construction, must be within the financial means of those expected to purchase it. Any non-monetary benefits will be relegated to second place if the financial requirements of a new stove are high.

Stoves made from unfired clay by the user are cheapest, but hardest to diffuse

Early stove programmes advocated stoves of unfired clay made by the user and her family members. They generally had low adoption rates, however. This resulted from the difficulties in diffusing design information to prospective users and maintaining fabrication of a sufficient standard. An alternative approach is to have improved stoves that are made and installed by local craftsmen. One example is the stove launched by the Sarvodaya Shranadana Movement in Sri Lanka. Potters were trained to make the stoves, and rural artisans were used to install them in the home (Shanahan, 1986, p. 72). However, it should be noted that the method of construction was not the only factor behind the success of stove dissemination in Sri Lanka. Additional favourable conditions included a strong dissemination structure, and interest by potters who were losing their conventional markets to aluminium pots.

The most successful projects have disseminated metal stoves in urban areas, where fuel is bought with cash

Stoves made from ceramic or metal have the advantage that they are usually portable, although those made from ceramic are heavier and more fragile. Stoves of this type, such as the metal *Jiko* of East Africa and *Feyu Malgache* found in many parts of the Sahel Africa, have been made by local artisans for decades. Similarly the *Thai bucket*, a ceramic stove with a metal liner, dates back to the 1920s (Bialy, 1986, p. 12; see also World Bank, 1986) and is found throughout Thailand. These stoves usually burn charcoal, although they can also be fuelled with wood and other biomass.

The most successful stove programmes have been where wood is purchased and have focused on urban or peri-urban areas and promoted metal stoves. In Kenya, for example, some 84,000 improved *Jiko* stoves costing between $4 and $6 were sold within 24 months (Hyman, 1986), and in Niger about 40,000 wood burning stoves made from scrap sheet metal were sold in the same period (Leach and Gowan, 1987, p. 67). These programmes have relatively centralized production and the stoves are distributed through local commercial channels. Buyers rely on cash savings from reduced wood and charcoal purchases to pay for the stove. While an important method of reducing wood consumption, it could only be replicated in relatively advanced rural areas where wood is sold.

In rural areas stove programmes should be integrated into other women's programmes

Experience has shown that in rural areas where there is little trade in wood it is easier to introduce stoves as part of a wider programme designed to improve the status of women and to raise the standard of health and hygiene. The Chinese stove programme is noteworthy, and as yet understudied. The key here is that the Chinese have extensive channels for transferring technology within and between rural areas.

The point of integrating stove projects into other women's programmes is that it reduces the amount of effort required to establish information channels on stoves, and looking at the totality of the problem prevents the imposition of unnecessary technological solutions. Changes in the design of kitchens and cooking practices may be just as important as new equipment. There are also reasons why certain practices are maintained: smoke from the fireplace repels mosquitoes and vermin; open fires give light (Gill, 1987). Without understanding the problems of women and the various opportunities for intervention, new stoves are unlikely to be of appropriate design.

The necessity of an energy transition

Rural wood markets are complex, and intervention is difficult

From the earlier discussion it will be clear that the rural fuelwood market in developing countries is complex. The rural household faces many sophisticated trade-offs in the choice of fuel. There is the choice of burning wood or agricultural residues. If wood is burnt, then long hours may have to be spent collecting it. If residues are burnt, soil fertility may fall and lead to a reduction in future crop yields. If the household owns trees, wood cut today is at the expense of wood consumption tomorrow. Wood may also have a cash value, and keeping the tree acts as a form of saving.

Moreover, the increasing wood scarcity in many regions may be having severe detrimental effects on some members of the rural community. Most particularly poor women may be having to carry heavy bundles of wood for long distances, and they may be having to use less preferred fuels that increase smoke in the kitchen. Diets may also be deteriorating if the choice of foodstuffs is influenced by the available cooking time.

The shift to different forms of energy can reduce woodfuel problems, both directly and indirectly

Interventions on the wood market are very difficult, because of the many interacting factors. Clearly, the need for wood is reduced if households or rural industries change from wood to other fuels such as kerosene, liquefied petroleum gas (LPG), and coke. Additionally, the adoption of new technologies for other rural activities can indirectly reduce the need to address woodfuel problems. The immediate problem for many families is the time that they must devote to collecting wood. This prevents them from doing other things that would provide income or increase family welfare. More trees and more efficient stoves are certainly two solutions. Within the list of activities that absorb family members' time, it is possible that other interventions would have a more rapid effect. One example is the installation of a village water supply, which may free women from having to carry water long distances and may have immediate health effects. Likewise, an increase in agricultural productivity may slow down the expansion of agricultural land and the destruction of forests.

These types of intervention require equipment: to pump water, for land preparation, for the treatment of produce, and for transportation of produce to markets. With rural mechanization comes the need for energy supplies to power the new machines. In this chapter the transfer to these new sources of energy is discussed in detail.

Kerosene as a household fuel

Kerosene is only used by the highest income groups in rural areas

As cash incomes increase there is a natural shift from wood to the so-called modern fuels of coke and kerosene (and perhaps LPG in areas close to cities). These fuels, particularly kerosene, are much more convenient to use than wood and other biomass fuels, but they are used for cooking only by the highest income groups in the rural areas of developing countries. It is interesting to note that even though kerosene is often considered to be more expensive than wood, a unit of heat from a kerosene stove may actually be cheaper than that obtained from wood. This is because the kerosene stove,with an efficiency of some 40 per cent, is perhaps 2.5 times as efficient as a woodstove (see World Bank, 1985b, for a summary of the technical characteristics of several kerosene stoves). Leach (1987, table 2.4) shows with price data from the Indian cities of Lucknow (in 1984) and Hyderabad (in 1985) that, if one ignores the cost of the stove, kerosene provided useful heat at approximately 45 per cent of the cost of wood.

Purchasing kerosene can pose cash-flow problems for poor families

Kerosene distribution networks in rural areas are often weak and inadequate so that either kerosene shortages occur, or a high mark-up must be paid to a few distributors. Surveys in the Pacific Island countries of Fiji, Kiribati and Tonga indicate that those families that cook mainly with kerosene use 4.2 to 5.6 litres per week per household. If the typical consumer of kerosene uses 4 litres per week of fuel, at an official price of the order of $0.40 per litre this requires $1.60, more than one day's wages for many labourers. The purchase of kerosene therefore poses cash-flow problems unless it is bought in very small quantities; but purchasing such small volumes can easily be double the official retail price.

The cost of a kerosene stove is often also a constraint for a similar reason. A kerosene stove may cost up to $5, equivalent to several days' income. The alternative of the three-stone wood fire has essentially no cost as it can be picked up from the ground. For a family with marginal cash incomes and no credit the choice of the latter is compelling.

If increasing the official price of kerosene led to more competition in distribution, then the rural retail price may actually fall

It has been suggested (e.g. by the World Bank, 1987a) that holding a subsidized price for kerosene is a direct cause of its limited availability in rural areas. Low kerosene prices limit the profitability of marketing this fuel. Oil companies with profit-maximizing goals would then minimize its distribution, especially in rural areas where transportation costs are high. Thus, it follows that increasing the controlled kerosene price could actually decrease the price in rural areas due to increased competition in the distribution phase.

The effect of price changes on demand depends upon the local situation

The effect this would have on consumption depends upon how much people change their purchases as the price changes, i.e. the price elasticity (which gives the percentage decrease in consumption for one percentage increase in price). No clear empirical evidence exists on the magnitudes of rural energy price elasticities. However, many observers comment that the transition between wood and kerosene is more strongly determined by income than by price (i.e. the price elasticity often appears to be very low). This is because the percentage of income spent on kerosene by the consumers that have the largest impact on the market is normally quite small (e.g. a few per cent) and because of the capital costs of appliances. This is illustrated by Table 3 which presents the results of a survey of urban consumers in Kenya. If the price elasticity was 1 for the lowest income group, 0.4 for the next lowest group, and 0.1 for the higher income groups, the response to an increase in the price of kerosene by 25 per cent would be to decrease the total consumption of kerosene by 5 per cent.

In the case of a country where three-quarters of kerosene consumption is in urban areas, typical of many low-income countries, an increase in the regulated price of kerosene by 50 per cent could reduce the retail price by 25 per cent in rural areas. Based upon the above elasticity assumptions, urban demand would fall by 10 per cent. Rural demand would have to increase by 30 per cent to maintain the same market volume, implying a price elasticity of more than 1 for rural consumers. It is apparent that the effects of increases in official price would require careful analysis at a local level before they can be recommended.

Table 3 Annual kerosene consumption and expenditures in urban Kenya by income group

Income groups (1979 $)	Percentage of households	Kerosene consumption (litres/year)	Percentage of total kerosene consumption	Kerosene expenditure as a percentage of income
0–410	5	76	3	11
411–1210	23	163	25	7
1211–2430	26	173	34	4
2431–7290	34	149	34	1
above 7290	12	49	4	—

Source: Compiled from tables 3.2 and 3.3; World Bank, 1987a.

The scarcity of foreign exchange will make the transfer to kerosene for cooking difficult

The constraints from limits on foreign exchange availability will also make the change from wood to kerosene an unpopular policy with the central planning authority. The quantity of kerosene that would be demanded by a household depends upon the number of family members and their income. It is incorrect to convert the wood currently consumed to kerosene on a heat value basis (i.e. one tonne of air dry wood is equivalent to 15 GJ which is equivalent to 0.35 tonnes of kerosene) because of the different stove efficiencies and changes in cooking practices.

Assuming an annual kerosene consumption of 50 kg per capita (i.e. 62 litres per annum per capita; a family of five would use 6 litres per week), a complete shift of one million people from wood to kerosene would cost $10 million each year at a kerosene price of $200 per tonne. To put this into context, if this shift were made by one-tenth of the population, the annual foreign exchange cost as a percentage of merchandise exports (1987 from World Bank, 1989) of the following countries would be:

59

Bangladesh	10 per cent
Burkina Faso	4 per cent
Burma	18 per cent
Burundi	6 per cent
Ethiopia	11 per cent
India	6 per cent
Madagascar	4 per cent
Mali	4 per cent
Mozambique	16 per cent
Nepal	12 per cent
Sudan	5 per cent
Tanzania	7 per cent

In a situation of economic austerity imposed by debt rescheduling the allocation of this magnitude of foreign exchange for cooking kerosene is implausible for much of highly indebted Africa. Furthermore, pressures from urban consumers makes an increase in the price of kerosene a politically costly route for the state. The government policy maker may legitimately argue that the welfare benefits to the rural poor are too doubtful to be counted in any decision. The main counter-argument to this is that in some situations growing wood can also have high costs.

Wood will remain a major fuel for the rural household for some time to come, although kerosene will be adopted naturally as incomes increase. Modern energy sources, if they are adopted, are more likely to be used for powering equipment, rather than as a substitute for wood.

Energy for agricultural mechanization

In addition to the possibility of using petroleum products to meet demands for domestic heat, modern forms of energy are also used for a variety of rural activities where shaft power is needed. Of course, this requires some type of engine or motor. Most of this demand comes from agriculture, although shaft power is needed by many rural industries.

Energy use in agriculture often does not receive sufficient attention by national planners

The use of petroleum products and electricity in agriculture often appears to be a very small proportion of the total national consumption of these items, and thus rural areas receive little attention by the energy ministry, while the agricultural ministry does not direct much effort to energy issues. In some cases this is a misrepresentation of statistics. For example, in Pakistan the Government's *Energy Year Book for 1985* states that agriculture is responsible for only 3 per cent of total national petroleum consumption. This is because, of all petroleum products, only the consumption of light diesel oil (which must be used in stationary low-speed engines) is attributed to agricultural activities: all other sales reported by petroleum distribution companies are allocated to the transportation sector.

A recent study of energy in Pakistan's agricultural sector estimated that as much as 45 per cent of all high-speed diesel oil may be used by tractors, and 20 per cent by irrigation pumps. This is equivalent to 30 per cent of total national petroleum consumption, and although tractors are used for transportation in addition to agriculture, it seems probable that the official statistics underestimate the share of agriculture to a large degree (deLucia and Associates, 1986).

Even if only small quantities of modern forms of energy are used in agriculture, this hides the fact that small quantities of energy can yield tremendous returns to farmers. This is most clearly the case when a new energy supply allows for a radical change in farming practices, such as when new 'green revolution' high-yielding crop varieties are adopted. For example, in northern India it has been estimated that irrigation with groundwater pumps leads to an increase in agricultural production as much as $600 per hectare (see Abbie *et al.*, 1982), but costs only $100 per hectare for a farmer operating 4 hectares (Hurst, 1985). This calculation was based on assumed economic costs, i.e. the true costs of the economy of pumping water. With subsidized energy prices, irrigation would be even more profitable, although it would be less attractive if credit were expensive (Lenoir, 1984, p. 45).

At the simplest levels of agriculture, only human labour and animals are used

Energy is used for several important agricultural activities (see Bhatia, 1984a; Makhijani and Poole, 1975; Reddy, 1985). Chronologically, this starts with land preparation, is followed by irrigation, harvesting, and then threshing and other post-harvest treatment. As farming systems change, the method of performing each of these activities also changes. At the simplest level only manpower is used, but as agriculture develops some animals are used along with people for land preparation. A large number of marginal and small farmers in developing countries fall into this category (CEEMAT, 1975; and Nolle).

At the next stage, small stationary engines are used for irrigation pumping and crop threshing

As the transition is made to modern energy, irrigation is usually the first activity to become mechanized. This is because traditional human- and animal-powered devices cannot normally provide sufficient water to allow the farmer to change the cropping pattern from that used under rainfed conditions; nor are they able to compensate for reductions in rainfall during drought. The additional control of water supply through mechanized irrigation usually permits the spread of crop planting through the year. Instead of growing only one major crop during the rainy season, double cropping becomes possible.

The demand for energy for irrigation is usually much larger than that for threshing

Often the same engine or motor used to pump water can also be used with simple mechanical threshers after the crops have been harvested. The amount of work required for threshing, oil extraction, and other mechanical crop processing is much less than that for irrigation. For example, it is typical to irrigate for about three months a year. Usually pumps are only run when people are in the fields, so the total number of hours of irrigation is approximately 800 to 900 hours per year (CEMAGREF, 1979).

Consider the example of a farmer with a 4-hectare farm. If a grain crop is irrigated, about 8 tonnes of grain could be produced when high-yielding crop varieties are planted and some commercial fertilizer applied. The engine used for irrigation (of between 3.75 and 5 kW) could also be used to thresh at least 1 tonne of grain per day. The total engine running time for crop processing would therefore be eight days, only some 60 to 70 hours.

In practice, the energy consumption of engines and motors may be much higher than expected owing to bad maintenance

Typically, engines used on farms are much less efficient than they need to be because of bad maintenance and incorrect engine adjustments. For example, in a survey of pumps in Gujarat, India (1979) Patel and Gupta estimated the efficiency of diesel pumpsets to be a mere 6 per cent. This compares with claims by Indian engine manufacturers of a fuel consumption of 1 litre per hour for a 3.75 kW diesel engine, an efficiency of about 30 per cent. With a pump of 50 per cent efficiency this would give an overall efficiency of 15 per cent. In practice, therefore, a diesel pump may have two-and-a-half times the expected fuel consumption. The reasons for this loss in performance (in no particular order) come from:

○ mis-matching of engines and pumps;

○ incorrect foot-valves in the wells;

○ incorrect pipe-work for irrigation water delivery;

○ improper lubrication;

○ faulty injectors;

○ worn out pistons and liners;

○ leaky valves;

○ the lack of fuel filters;

○ worn out bearings;

○ faulty exhaust piping;

○ faulty governors.

The efficiency of electric motors is also often less than it should be. In this case the losses come from incorrect sizing of motors. When running at its optimal load an electric motor (excluding the pump) should have an efficiency of between 80 per cent (for 3 kW) and 90 per cent (for 15 kW). At a partial load of 75 per cent of the rated capacity, about 10 per cent of power consumption is wasted, and this loss increases at a rapid rate as the loading decreases. If pumps are damaged they are sometimes rewound in local workshops. If poor quality copper wire with unsuitable insulation is used, the efficiency of a motor can fall to below 50 per cent (deLucia and Associates, 1986). With this combination of factors, electricity consumption could again be more than double that expected.

However, it should be remembered that motors with excess capacity have the advantage that they can at times be run at much higher rates than normal. If the motor or its attachments break down, a larger-than-needed motor may be able to compensate for lost production once repaired.

Projects should ensure that new equipment can be correctly maintained. Excess energy supply capacity should also be installed

Projects that introduce engines and motors must ensure that proper maintenance facilities are available. If these are not established, a much larger supply of energy may have to be provided. *As a rule of thumb it can be assumed that a diesel pumpset will consume approximately 1.33 litres of diesel oil for every kWh* (this is a 10 per cent overall efficiency). It is common for pumps to be over-sized for usual operations, and to be run at partial load.

Small farmers with excess engine capacity can also thresh crops for other farmers who do not possess engines. For example, in North Bihar, India Clay (1982) observes that some small farmers with diesel pumpsets set up service businesses that thresh grain along roadsides. The introduction of mobile pumpsets may therefore have a negative impact on employment for threshing. This is a loss of between 10 and 16 person-days per tonne.

However, land preparation is still done with animals and people, and harvesting continues to use human labour. The demand for these activities can increase as crop yields increase in response to controlled irrigation.

At the next stage of agricultural development, land preparation becomes mechanized with tractors and power tillers

The next major change occurs when land preparation becomes mechanized. This can be done with small power tillers or with tractors. By much reducing the time for ploughing and tilling they permit further changes to the cropping pattern, and possibly triple cropping of the same piece of land each year. For example, a pair of bullocks working six hours per day would take five days to plough one hectare (Hurst, 1983). Animals cannot work in the sun for a greater number of hours per day without becoming overheated. By comparison, a 7.5 kW power tiller should be able to plough one hectare in eight hours (Sanghi and Blase, 1976, Table II), while a 20 kW tractor would take 2.5 hours per hectare (Biggs and Burns, 1977, p. 84). Usually fields are ploughed several times prior to crop planting (e.g. six to eight ploughings have been observed for rice and wheat in India). A tractor with a suitable range of implements can be used for the complete range of agricultural activities.

The effects of tractors on agricultural productivity, employment and income distribution are unclear. There is much debate over the benefits of tractorization. Its opponents argue that the use of tractors has negative impacts on income distribution and employment, and is a misallocation of scarce capital and foreign exchange. Even when compensating jobs are created, it is argued that there is an increased seasonability of employment which provides a stimulus for further mechanization. There may also be indirect labour displacement through tenant eviction as mechanized holdings expand in pursuit of economies of scale.

There is also uncertainty over the extent to which tractorization increases agricultural profits. Barker *et al.* (1973), for example, in a study of Laguna in the Philippines, infer that increased yields were largely attributable to the use of high-yield crop varieties, better weeding, fertilizer application, and the more regular supply of water, rather than to the use of tractors. Studies of this issue often use regression analysis in an attempt to identify the effects of tractors on agricultural production (see Binswanger, 1978, for citations) and a common result is that tractors have little effect on the productivity of land and a negative effect on employment.

Other commentators have argued that the bulk of time devoted to draught animals is for generally looking after them rather than for ploughing. As Desai (1982) observed in Punjab, India, this was done mostly with family labour, which was not released from employment when tractors were used, but was re-absorbed in looking after an increased number of buffaloes and cows kept for milk production.

Tractor use will continue to grow

Even if in many locations tractors largely substitute animals and labour with capital, it is true that tractors are used in many countries. In some areas there are animal power constraints, and here tractors do permit an (albeit capital-intensive) increase in yields.

It should also be noted that the use of animals for work acts as a drain on rural resources. On average, only about 30 per cent (on a dry weight basis) of fodder eaten by cattle is returned to the soil in their dung (see Desai, 1980). As a consequence, it is possible that the continual intensification of agriculture with animals would have a cost in terms of soil fertility.

The possible extent of this can be seen with the example of Bangladesh. In this country the second Five Year Plan (1980) stated that there was a shortfall of about two million draught animals nationwide for development needs. Gill (1983b) estimates that nearly 50 thousand power tillers would be needed to replace these animals. The value of diesel oil to run these tillers is equivalent to 93 thousand tonnes of fertilizer, and the capital required is equivalent to 455 thousand tonnes (ibid, p. 342). Annualizing capital costs at a 10 per cent discount rate over ten years gives a total foreign exchange cost of power tillers of 170 thousand tonnes of fertilizer per year. This is a major foreign exchange requirement.

In a country such as Bangladesh, most fodder for animals comes from cultivated land. If animals only return to the field two-thirds of the nitrogen in their fodder, the drain of two million animals would be equivalent to 23 thousand tonnes of fertilizer (i.e. urea). Allowing some food consumption for female animals and calves (needed to maintain the male draft population) this increases to 50 thousand tonnes of fertilizer, approximately one-third of the cost of power tillers.

It would be quite legitimate to challenge the assumptions used in this calculation. However, the figures do show that using animals can have some, possibly significant, cost for the rural environment. This follows a similar logic to that applied to the burning of agricultural residues as a household fuel, although it is perhaps less expected. Overgrazing of fallow land can also lead to severe environmental problems from soil erosion.

Whatever the pros and cons of tractors, their introduction is something which appeals to international aid organizations. The stock of tractors is likely to continue to increase rapidly from the 1983 level of about 2.5 million in developing countries (FAO, 1983, p. 64). For reference it is estimated that some 280 million head of domestic animals are used to supply draught power (FAO, 1983, p. 83).

Tractors may work for about half the year, but only at a fraction of the rated capacity of the engine

These farm implements are usually sized at between 7.5 kW for small tillers to about 50 kW for tractors, although some more powerful tractors are used. The fuel consumption of a tractor depends upon the type of work that it is doing. Estimates in Pakistan put the diesel oil consumption of a 40kW tractor at about 5 litres per hour. If the engine efficiency were 20 per cent this would mean that the tractor engine is on average producing 10 kW, about a quarter of its rated load.

It has also been estimated in Pakistan that the average running time for tractors for all purposes, including their use for transportation, is about seven hours per day for 200 days per year (Pakistan Census of Agricultural Machinery, 1975). This is a total running time of 1400 hours per year, and an annual fuel consumption of 7000 litres per tractor. Tractors that are not being used by the owners are often rented to others, thus maintaining this relatively high utilization rate.

Reliability of energy supplies

The adoption of new technologies requires the farmer to make major decisions. Each of the above agricultural transitions involves many changes in farmer behaviour (see Binswanger, 1984). Firstly, the appropriate equipment must be purchased. The necessary inputs to keep the equipment operating must be secured, i.e. an energy supply, maintenance, and spare parts. The farmer must then adjust his or her crop planting in order to benefit from the purchase. These are major changes in customs and traditional practices, and it is natural for farmers to be cautious in making such decisions. The credit available to small farmers may be primarily from expensive informal sources. In order to maintain loan repayments, the success of the new pump or tiller will need to be almost a certainty. In the extreme, when a farmer grows new crops that are very sensitive to irrigation, the failure of a pump at a crucial time of plant growth could mean the loss of the crop and complete ruin for the farmer. (There is a large literature on the degree of risk aversion of farmers including Lipton, 1968; Scandizzo and Dillon, 1979; Wolgin, 1975; Michailof, 1987, p. 31.)

A reliable energy supply is needed to reduce the risks of purchasing new equipment

Together with the other requirements for maintenance, a guaranteed supply of energy is very important in reducing the riskiness of the purchase of new technology (see Hurst, 1986). This is often overlooked in development projects. For example, agricultural development projects can include diesel engines without properly studying the supply of diesel oil. The fact that diesel oil is available in some nearby city does not necessarily mean that it will be available to the farmer. The distribution network for petroleum products in rural areas are often very weak, and the farmer may have to pay a large mark-up over the city price. Even if the average local price is not much above the urban price, the supply may be very variable. During the rains when roads become impassable by

66

motor vehicles the price of diesel may increase by orders of magnitude. Fortunately, the need for irrigation or tillage at this time will usually be at a minimum.

Similar problems arise with rural electrification. The pressure from the energy ministry on the electric utility is usually to electrify as many villages as possible. This means that investments in the reliability of electricity supply are sacrificed for an extensive grid network. The low price for electricity charged to rural consumers can also mean that the utility does not develop rural markets in an efficient manner, and simply strings lines to fulfil the directives of the central government.

The supply options to meet agricultural energy demands are discussed later. It is important to note that the demand for energy depends upon the prior purchase of appliances, and the purchase of complementary inputs to make the appliances productive. Most of all it depends upon the perceived reliability of the purchases made and of the energy supply chosen. Without proper maintenance the energy demand of these appliances can easily double. Unless sufficient supply capacity is available to deal with this increase in demand there can be energy supply shortages.

Energy projects should be incorporated into other agricultural development projects

As with woodfuel projects, it follows that to improve the chances of success, energy projects should be integrated with other projects to increase and manage energy demand. These include irrigation projects, agricultural extension projects, rural credit schemes, and technical and vocational training projects. Similarly the success of other projects is more likely if energy supply is carefully considered: many agricultural projects need energy.

Energy for rural industries

'. . . rural industry should be promoted each time it is technically practicable. This implies four main conditions:

- ○ a political will to stimulate and protect a rural industry which would be unable to compete with conventional industry or imports without protection (taxation and customs policies, favourable credit policies, subsidies and adapted wages policies);

- ○ . . . the availability of energy supplies and more often of electricity;

- ○ choosing to simplify processes and products . . .;

- ○ deciding to orientate industrial sub-contracting towards the countryside . . .'

(Michailof, 1987, p. 187).

67

Many rural industries treat agricultural produce; some require shaft power

Many rural industries process agricultural commodities. Some of these are large factories that buy produce from many farmers. Others involve only the on-farm crop processing of the production of a particular farmer and his or her immediate neighbours.

Those activities that require shaft power normally use diesel engines or electric motors, and much of the discussion of pumps and threshers of the last section applies. The larger the quantity of produce treated, the larger the engine or motor used, although the capacity does not go above 35 kW in most cases. Examples include cotton ginning, rice milling, sugar processing, and coffee hulling.

Some crop processing requires heat

Many rural industries also require heat. It was observed in the section on woodfuel that these can often use large quantities of wood in a particular location. For example, heat is required during tea production to dry the leaves after withering and fermentation. Typical wood consumption rates are 3.0 tonnes to 4.5 tonnes per tonne of tea produced. Tobacco is also dried prior to sale, and sometimes this is done in heated barns. These barns are heated either by placing them over a furnace, or by circulating hot air from a heat exchanger. Fuel consumption varies tremendously from 10 to 100 tonnes of wood per tonne of tobacco (data from FAO internal documents but see also Barnard and Zaror, 1986).

Demands for heat are often met with wood; modern forms of energy can also be used, but only if the price of wood rises sufficiently

In these and other cases of drying, wood could be replaced with diesel oil or coal. Because of their relative energy content one tonne of wood could be replaced by half a tonne of coal or one-third of a tonne of diesel oil. However, wood-fuelled drying itself can be made more efficient: a range of 0.7 to 2.5 tonnes of wood per tonne of tea has been reported in some plantations with modern driers (Gilmour *et al.*, 1987). In some industries, biomass wastes are produced that can be used as a fuel. A major example is the use of bagasse in the boilers of sugar plants (Rivière, 1987).

However, many agricultural by-products are not easy to handle. They have a very low density which makes them expensive to move and store unless they are first pelletized or densified. This treatment is also required for some biomass fuels if they are to burn in a controlled manner and deliver heat at a sufficient rate. Other agricultural by-products, such as rice husks, contain silica which causes slagging in furnaces.

The transfer to modern energy will only happen if it is economically attractive to make the change. Wood is often very cheap, and the situations will be limited where people managing crop processing will purchase oil products and burners. As with the rural household, wood will be the major fuel for generating heat for some time to come.

Solar driers can be used to dry crops

Many crops are dried simply by laying them on mats in the sun. An alternative that has been proposed is the use of solar driers. These work on the same principle as a greenhouse. A description of solar driers is given in the report *Drying of Food Products in the Developing Countries* published by the Directorate General for Development of the Commission of the European Communities. The ILO (1986b) study on solar driers includes a large bibliography.

It is argued that solar driers allow more rapid drying in controlled conditions. Further, they permit drying in adverse climatic conditions. In regions where there is mechanized agriculture and double or triple cropping, crops may be harvested in the rainy season (e.g. Thailand). Here solar driers may result in significant crop savings. In areas of lower rainfall, where there is just one crop, only a small proportion of post-harvest losses may result from inadequate drying, and the benefits of solar driers will be less.

Effective drying is most valuable with vegetables, fruit and fish

The best returns for these devices come with high-value produce that have a high water content and so are susceptible to deterioration. Examples are vegetables, fruit and fish. Indeed solar driers are used in large-scale operations in Argentina, Brazil, Greece, Israel, Portugal and Turkey for drying fruit such as figs, raisins, and dates.

The drying of fish in solar driers is an alternative method of preservation to fish smoking. Smoking is usually done at a family level in ovens holding from 50 to 500 kg of fish. The time required depends upon the type of fish and the quality of the produce: wood consumption for smoking varies between 2 and 12 tonnes per tonne of fish (data from FAO internal documents).

There may not be much demand for better quality solar-dried produce outside the large cities

Smoking fish gives a characteristic taste which is not the case with solar-dried fish. Nonetheless, it is argued that the public prefer solar-dried fish to air-dried fish because of the reduced risk of spoilage and infestation from insects. However, in Senegal, where some solar-dried fish are produced, merchants sell them mixed together with traditionally dried fish as no price differential (Ward *et al.*, 1984). It is extremely unlikely that fish traders would not set different prices for solar-dried fish if a higher price could be obtained. Therefore, it is likely that many people do not wish to pay more for better quality fish. In order to reach markets where there is a demand for the premium quality of fish that have been solar dried may mean taking the fish to larger towns (i.e. from *inelastic* to *elastic* markets). The attractiveness of a solar drier will depend upon the access to transportation to cities. Similar arguments apply to other solar-dried produce (Pereira, 1985).

Some driers are most suitable with large concerns, where good quality driers can be afforded

There have also been some problems in the fabrication of cheap but reliable designs of solar driers. Earlier designs using polythene sheeting were unsuccessful due to colouration of the polythene by ultra-violet light. Metal-framed driers are expensive, but artisanal fabrications from wood have not been robust enough or had sufficiently good seals (Ward *et al.*, 1984). Consequently, solar driers are most likely to succeed for large-scale operations, where relatively expensive and reliable designs can be used. Here they would substitute for drying in sunlight, and in a few cases with wood (as with tea and tobacco discussed above).

Brickmaking is one of the most energy-intensive rural industries

Some of the most energy intensive of rural industries are those that fire clay for bricks and pottery. The simplest and most widespread method of firing bricks is the clamp kiln. This involves stacking the freshly made green bricks over a wood bed which is then lit: it is in effect nothing more than a pile of bricks over a wood fire. Since little can be done to control the burning of the fuel, and heat transfer through the bricks can be irregular, the process is inefficient in energy use and can lead to bricks of variable quality.

A variation is the scove kiln which has outside walls of fired (stacked, but uncemented) bricks. More complicated kilns include permanent walls of bricks and mortar (e.g. the Scotch kiln) and sometimes permanent roofs. They are still operated on a batch basis with the bricks being stacked in the kiln, fired, and then removed. A description of brickmaking in developing countries can be found in Baily (1980), Hill (1980), ILO (1984), and Keddie and Cleghorn (1980). Pottery kilns operate on the same principles, but are smaller than brick kilns.

More efficient brickmaking technology is found in South Asia

In India and Pakistan the Bull's Trench kiln is also widely used to fire bricks. It involves a circular trench approximately 100m in circumference in which the green bricks are stacked. The top is covered with ash and rubble to make an air seal. Wood is fed into the kiln through ports in the side so that the fire slowly moved around the circular trench. A metal chimney is placed over a hole in the top covering and is also moved around the kiln a few metres in front of the fire. The kiln can be operated in a continuous process with fired and cooled bricks (on the opposite side of the circle from the fire) being removed and new green bricks added. The advantage of this continuous operation is that waste heat from the fire is used to dry bricks before the fire approaches (— the point of having the metal chimney ahead of the fire as it moves around the circle), thus reducing the heat required for firing.

A brickworks will consume as much energy as hundreds of households

A clamp kiln can burn between one and four kilograms of wood per brick: a small brickmaker producing 1000 bricks per day would need between 350 and 1400 tonnes of wood per year, perhaps the same amount as 100 to 400 households. The more efficient Bull's Trench kiln reduces the wood burnt per brick to as little as a quarter of that for the clamp. The size of the circular trench for practical operation means that many more bricks must be made. Currently they need to contain 250,000 bricks and fire 50,000 per day. For this size of Bull's Trench kiln the annual wood consumption will be at least 5,000 tonnes per year (data from internal World Bank reports). However, other fuels, such as coal, may be used when production reaches these levels.

The change to modern fuels will require the adoption of completely new kilns in most countries

Energy costs are a major proportion of the total costs for brickmakers. The ILO (1984, p. 174–75) calculate for small-scale brick production in Tanzania that 48 per cent of costs are for labour, 43 per cent for wood, and the remainder to cover other materials and capital. Therefore, there is an incentive for brickmakers to consider alternative sources of energy.

Brickmakers could shift to modern forms of energy. In general this requires a permanent kiln. Clamp kilns very rarely use anything but wood, although the scove kiln is fuelled with oil in a few counties. The Bull's Trench kiln generally has a permanent location, and in Pakistan it is fuelled with coal and natural gas if it is available. Rural brickmakers using the clamp design, the most common method in Africa, will normally have to build new kilns before modern energy sources will be used.

Projects that promote rural industries must consider an energy dimension

Rural industries are a key to rural development. They generate value-added in rural areas, and increase linkages with urban markets. For those industries using mechanical work, energy costs are usually a relatively small component of total costs. However, a supply of energy to power engines and motors is a necessary component for these activities.

Many rural industries require heat, and wood is the major fuel. Here the energy costs may be large, but the transfer to modern energy may involve a substantial technical change and capital investment. Although the relative importance of energy may be reduced, total costs will be increased. This problem is exacerbated by the low price paid by rural industries for wood in many areas.

Energy for rural transport

The economics of rural industries often depend upon the quality of rural transportation services

The demand for rural industries is highy influenced by the availability of rural transport. This is needed both to carry raw materials and fuel to the rural enterprise, and to take the final product to market centres in towns.

Many different forms of transport are used (see Beenhakker *et al.*, 1987; Carapetis *et al.*, 1984; Barwell *et al.*, 1985; AFME, 1984). Goods are carried by people, on animal carts, by tractor, and on trucks. In small island countries, boats are often the major form of transportation. Government interventions to improve the availability of rural transport can take many forms. The most common is investment in road infrastructure.

Transportation with animals on tracks is common — many people may not have access to modern transport on good roads

It is important to note that in rural areas much transportation takes place with non-motorized vehicles on fine-weather roads, small tracks, and trails. Major all-weather roads may not reach many, and a bias towards building them may be of little help to a large proportion of the rural population. Additionally, the income of small industries (e.g. family-level crop processing and fish smoking) may be such that they cannot afford the fares charged by large trucks operating along these roads.

Other policies include the improvement of traditional animal-drawn carts. This can mean the introduction of improved steel axles, the use of pneumatic tyres, and better harnesses for animals (see Hathaway, 1985). Such projects involve the diffusion of technical information and credit schemes to finance alterations. If the animal population is not sufficient to support an increase in the demand for transportation, motor cycles and small motorized three-wheeled vehicles are often more suitable than large trucks.

The relative importance of transportation in rural diesel oil consumption depends upon the degree of rural mechanization

If rural industries are developed, the availability of rural transport requires detailed study. Indeed, a transportation system is required to bring diesel oil and spare parts for the equipment used by rural industries and farmers. Transportation using trucks and tractors requires diesel oil, but the demand is usually smaller than for agriculture or rural industries. Returning to our hypothetical example of a farmer cultivating four hectares of grain, the following diesel oil requirements would exist:

○ irrigation for 800 hours with a 3.75 kW diesel engine at a 65 per cent load factor (which would pump about 44,000 cubic metres of water through a lift of 10m, enough for four hectares of rice) would require 2000 litres of diesel oil;

○ the use of a tractor for 50 hours of ploughing, land preparation, and other activities would require 250 litres of diesel oil;

○ the use of a thresher for 60 hours (with the 3.75 kW diesel engine operating at a 50 per cent load factor) would consume 100 litres of diesel oil;

○ five 30 km trips to market by tractor might use 50 litres of diesel oil (i.e. 3 km per litre).

The breakdown of energy consumption will be dramatically different for other agricultural produce. Sugar-cane, for example, may not be irrigated, but produces 30 to 50 tonnes of cane per hectare, and much more transportation to sugar plants would be needed. Treatment of sugar-cane to produce sugar is also energy intensive, although the cane provides most of this energy itself.

The energy component of rural transportation should not be forgotten

The importance of transportation as a consumer of diesel oil energy depends upon the level of mechanization of agriculture and rural industries. It would usually be a small part of a project that introduced groundwater pumping or tractors, but it would have greater importance for projects that focus on rural industries alone.

Adequate transportation is an essential component to rural development. Although it may be a minor part of a transportation project, appropriate energy infrastructure to support motorized transport should not be ignored.

Energy for social projects

Modern forms of energy may also be necessary for some social sector projects that provide for the needs of rural people. The most common activities that directly need these forms of energy are:

○ village water supply;

○ rural health centres;

○ village lighting.

Village water supply requires small quantities relative to agriculture. It can be provided with several handpumps, or with a mechanical pump and a central water tank

The quantities of water used for drinking, cooking and washing by rural people is much smaller than that used for irrigation. At a consumption of 30 litres per person per day, a village of 1000 people would consume 11,000 cubic metres of water per year, about the same as a hectare of rice, or four hectares of wheat.

Pumping of ground water provides a convenient supply of water in many areas. The major options are to install several small handpumps, or to build a storage tank to serve an entire village and have some form of mechanized pumping. In the latter case one small engine would be sufficient for most villages. It should also be remembered that the collection and storage of rain water is an energy-free alternative that can be cost effective. The topic of village water supply is discussed in detail by Saunders and Warford (1976) and World Bank (1987c).

The organization of effective pump operation and maintenance is important for success

An important issue with community projects is the organization of pump maintenance. In India the programme of installation of handpumps has been very successful. Here the costs of installing the pumps are covered by the government. The villagers are responsible for choosing one person to be trained as a pump technician. The government also provides a skilled mechanic for every 100 pumps, and repair and maintenance facilities at a district level.

The maintenance and operation of single pumps that fill a village water tank can be more complex depending upon the pumping technology installed. If diesel engines are used then someone must also be responsible for procuring diesel oil and ensuring that it is used in the pump. Some renewable energy technologies, e.g, windmills, are often suggested as an appropriate alternative. The attraction of introducing new technologies with this type of project is that the choice of equipment is made by project managers who also cover the capital costs of the equipment installed. This does not eliminate problems of maintenance, however.

The technical options for providing shaft power are discussed further in the next section. A detailed discussion is also available in the report *Renewable Sources of Energy and Village Water Supply in Developing Countries* published by the Directorate General for Development of the Commission of the European Communities.

Rural health centres require small but extremely reliable quantities of electricity

In rural health centres, energy is needed to power refrigerators for vaccines, and to sterilize medical equipment. Again the demands of energy are very small. Refrigerators for the storage of medication and electric heaters for sterilization need no more than a few kW at most. As the shelf life of many vaccines at room temperature is short, an extremely reliable supply of electricity is needed for refrigerators (Haentjens and Maillard, 1985).

Use of conventional energy alternatives is expensive. One would need a diesel generator, a back-up system in case of breakages, and a large inventory of diesel oil to cope with fuel shortages. Because of this, alternatives such as photovoltaic systems are often advocated. Another Commission document, *Energy and Health Care in the Developing Countries*, also discusses this topic in much more detail.

Hot water is also needed in health centres

In addition to refrigeration, hot water is required in health centres to maintain satisfactory levels of cleanliness. It can be heated on woodstoves, with electric immersion heaters, and with solar water heaters. Solar water heaters would have few other applications in rural areas, although they are used in cities in numerous countries (see Bruggink, 1984; Hurst 1986; and SIDA 1984 for more details).

Electricity in rural areas can be needed for electric lighting, telecommunications, and navigational beacons

Village electrification is also often justified as a social amenity because of the good lighting that it can provide. Again the demand for electricity is extremely low for this purpose. At the true costs of providing electric light alone there would be essentially no demand by rural people. The improvement in lighting of electric bulbs over oil lamps is simply not valued sufficiently to justify the required cash outlays. The use of electric lighting depends upon the overall policy regarding the electrification of rural areas.

Small-scale electricity generation is also sometimes needed for telecommunications and for navigational beacons. Again a very reliable supply of electricity is needed. In these cases the costs of providing electricity are always covered by the central government. Some of the technical options are discussed in the CEC report *Electric Power for Equipment in Remote Areas in Developing Countries.*

Conventional energy supplies

There are many technically feasible methods of meeting rural energy demands, and this section will not dwell on the different designs, efficiencies, and costs, but will give some introductory comments on the general suitability of each technology. At present the most common forms of modern energy in rural areas are diesel oil and electricity.

Petroleum products are needed for some rural activities

Rural transportation and land preparation requires either people, animals, or engines fuelled with petroleum products. The diesel pumpset and small diesel-electric generator are to be found in many areas. The need to consider the distribution of petroleum products to rural areas as part of a development project is obvious. Several important points regarding rural petroleum markets are worth reiterating in the discussion of this section.

Policies for the retailing of petroleum products in rural areas are highly dependent on national policies that respond to international markets and urban demand

As with other aspects of rural development, policies for the provision of petroleum products to rural areas are highly influenced by national policies oriented primarily to urban consumers and industries. These policies are, in turn, constrained by macroeconomic factors, the structure of international oil markets, and the technical capabilities of the oil industry in the country in question. While the international trade in small volumes of petroleum products may be unprofitable, the refineries operated within a particular country may produce products in proportions that are not compatible with national demand. The actions of government planners are often directed towards these national questions, rather than on the issues of developing new markets (although this is not always the case, particularly in some Pacific countries).

Oil companies are usually not interested in developing rural petroleum product markets

Similar biases exist in the oil companies operating in developing countries, be they national or transnational. Within oil companies the prestige staff positions are those involved in negotiating contracts for the international trade in crude oil, or concession terms for exploration and field development.

Moreover, the economics of the rural petroleum market with its highly dispersed consumers, each with a small individual demand, are not

76

attractive for an oil distribution company. Demand is, of course, a function of price, and low subsidized prices may be needed to make petroleum affordable to rural people. However, it means that the profits from the sale of petroleum products can be very small, or even negative. Weak regulation and a lack of competitive supply can mean that small quantities of fuel are sold at a considerable premium over official prices by small traders. However, these volumes are too small to create interest by an oil company (see earlier discussion on household use of kerosene).

Investments in petroleum supply include new depots, trucks, and retail outlets. Improving the efficiency of petroleum use is also important

As a result of a lack of investment in supply infrastructure, the availability of petroleum products in rural areas is usually variable and uncertain. Particularly during the rainy season when rural transportation becomes difficult, there can be long periods of shortage. Even short distances from town petroleum products may not be readily available. Consequently all projects that will require oil products to be used by the rural population should consider investments in new supply depots, new trucks for oil distribution, and new retail outlets.

In the discussion of agricultural mechanization it was noted that the efficiency of diesel engines in rural areas is often low. Programmes to improve the fuel use in such appliances can greatly assist in alleviating petroleum product supply constraints.

Rural electrification usually is a major component of rural energy plans

Rural electrification has a special place in the provision of energy to rural areas. This is because electricity is identified with the general modernization of rural areas. Electricity can meet many demands for energy, and is often technically the most appealing. Electric motors can be used for any application where a stationary motor is needed. In addition it can supply lighting to homes and villages; however, electricity is rarely economic for cooking or transportation.

Nearly all governments advocate rural electrification, and have projects to electrify villages. In the case of Bangladesh it is actually written in the constitution that electricity will at some stage be provided to all Bangladeshis. However, electricity distribution requires large quantities of capital and, whatever the wish, electricity will not reach many people in their lifetime (Maillard & Vernet, 1985).

Rural electricity supplied from a centralized utility has some unique features.

The special feature of expansion of the electricity grid is that large rural investments must be made by a centralized utility. This is also true of the distribution of petroleum products, but to a much lesser extent. One potential advantage of an energy supply managed by a central organization is that maintenance of the distribution system can also be centralized with trained specialist technicians.

Another potential advantage of electricity is that electric appliances are usually cheaper. Put another way, a larger proportion of the total capital investment of consuming energy is covered by the utility. The lower capital outlay by consumers reduces the need for loans, and reduces the difficulties in obtaining credit. Indeed, a lack of access to credit often severely limits the extent to which rural people can pursue their own independent energy supply options.

However, the economics of rural electrificatrion are often poor. This is because of many factors. The demand for electricity in rural areas for lighting and small electric motors is low; load factors are also low, typically about 10 per cent compared with 40 per cent in urban areas; there are high levels of power losses because of inadequate maintenance and, to a lesser extent, theft (e.g. in Pakistan, Tendler (1979) puts this at 35 per cent of power generation); and rural villages are dispersed, making distribution costs high. The end result is that the electric utility often requires large subsidies from outside the rural area for it to generate affordable electricity. The economics of rural electrification is discussed at length by Munasinghe, 1987 (see also World Bank, 1975).

Many benefits are attributed to rural electrification

The list of potential benefits attributed to rural electrification is often very long. The possible economic benefits include an increase in agricultural production and greater rural industrialization. Other linkages with the rural economy could include an increase in manufacturing activity to supply components for the electric utility such as poles and lines.

The non-financial benefits that can occur include an increase in the quality of rural life and a reduced migration to cities. Indeed, the numerous benefits attributed to the spread of the electric light includes all kinds of aspects of rural life. These usually focus on morally approvable changes such as improved homework by students, and evening group social activities, rather than the growth in night-time bars, clubs, and the video porn industry.

Rural electrification does not lead automatically to development

However, there is little evidence to suggest that rural electricity is a precondition to rural development, or indeed that it acts as a catalyst for development. Fluitman (1983, p. 25–26) describes the process of rural electrification as follows:

78

'on the conventional wisdom that rural electrification is a good thing, a political decision is taken to the effect that a significant amount of money should be mobilized and used to extend the electricity grid . . .; the decision, handed down to an organization responsible for implementing rural electrification programmes, is translated into nuts and bolts; sometimes, particularly if external fund are to be used, an attempt is made at cost-benefit analysis; but . . . conceptual and measurement problems cause costs to be under-estimated while demand for the service, and hence the benefits, tend to be over-estimated; if the resulting rate of return is nonetheless too low, immeasurable benefits, usually including the political returns on which the decision was based in the first place, are invoked, and the project approved; its success is measured in the numbers of electrified villages; the project is finally completed and the utility starts to make heavy losses; after some time, particularly if external funds have been used, an impact study of one sort or another is undertaken . . .; unfortunately the study suffers from the well-known measurement problems and is therefore inconclusive; the rural electrification programme is expanded to cover more remote areas where fewer and poorer people live; additional subsidies take care of the ever-increasing losses'.

Rural electrification must compete with distorted energy prices. This restricts the financial viability of these projects

This pessimistic view undoubtedly holds true in many regions, but must be taken with some provisos. Firstly, petroleum products can substitute for electricity in rural areas. Rural industries and farmers irrigating large areas will shift from electricity if it is an uncompetitive fuel; but diesel oil is often subsidized and so subsidies on electricity may be necessary. This does not reflect an unsuitability of rural electrification investments *per se*, but rather highly distorted energy prices.

Nonetheless, rural electrification will be a major component of rural energy supply investments

Furthermore, the capital costs of electrification are often covered by foreign assistance. It is likely that bilateral aid organizations will continue to disburse funds for rural electrification. Indeed, donors may find rural electrification projects an easy way of disbursing large funds. Although rates of return may be very low, it does not follow that the same funds would be available at the same terms for investment in other more profitable infrastructure. This, combined with political pressures within recipient countries, will mean that the area under rural electrification is certainly going to continue to expand. In a situation where rural electrification is going ahead anyway, the task of the adviser may be to assure that the least uneconomic option is chosen.

Reliability of electricity supply is a key issue

Reliability of energy supply is often sacrificed in a decision-making process that emphasizes extension to new areas, rather than market development. Power blackouts are common in developing countries. Indeed, in some areas farmers use electric pumps because they are the most cost-effective method of pumping water, but keep back-up diesel pumpsets for times when electricity is not available.

The optimal choice of power station, the plant capacities and energy sources utilized, may be quite different from the present investment strategies if the current loss of load probability is decreased in rural areas. For example, smaller, more geographically dispersed power stations, including small hydro power, may play a larger role. See *Rural Electrification in Developing Countries* (another Commission document prepared by the Directorate General for Development) for a further discussion of the options.

The effectiveness of rural electrification projects can be improved by appropriate project design. This includes personnel planning

Because the diffusion of suitable electric appliances is needed to complement rural electrification, special attention should be paid to the mechanisms that will provide this equipment. Interventions may include the creation of extension services to potential customers to help establish an electricity market (possibly including NGOs). The management of demand is equally important. For example, inefficiencies in electric appliances from having excessively sized motors can be corrected through the fitting of capacitors. This can reduce peak supply capacity requirements and save substantial investment expenditure for the utility. These extension services and other manpower training issues are discussed by ILO (1983).

Renewable energy technologies

Renewable technologies use energy sources available in the rural location. Examples are photovoltaics, windmills, micro-hydro power, biogas plants, and gasifiers. As with electricity they are technically feasible for most stationary applications. They have often been an important component of rural energy plans. Many programmes of foreign assistance have installed renewable technologies, although very few have gone beyond the demonstration and pilot project stage. In general, successful programmes have resulted more from material efforts than from foreign assistance projects.

A detailed economic and technical description of the alternatives is beyond the scope of this guide, but a few observations on each technology are given below.

Photovoltaics

Photovoltaics (PV) arrays are perhaps the most technically elegant of all energy sources, generating electricity from sunlight with no moving parts. Unfortunately, they are extremely expensive, costing about $4 per peak Watt. Under typical sunlight found in the tropics a one-peak-kilowatt system would in practice generate approximately 5 kWh per day.

A photovoltaic system has other components. In the case of water pumping it requires an electric motor, a pump, and other ancillary equipment. These cost about $5 extra per peak Watt of array. Given that electricity is generated during daylight hours, expensive storage batteries may be needed to run appliances.

Advocates of this technology argue that technical change in the production process of photovoltaic cells is taking place, and that the price will fall rapidly in the near future. While the price is decreasing, the actual fall in price has lagged a long way behind anticipations. A typical prediction is that by the mid-1990s prices will fall to between $1 and $2 per peak Watt for the array, and $3 per peak Watt for a pumping system.

The advantage of photovoltaics is that they can come in very small sizes, and costs are more or less linear with capacity. Therefore, they can often generate electricity competitively with electrical supply from diesel generators (which do not come in sizes below 2 to 3 kW) at small capacities. Nonetheless, this is expensive electricity, and photovoltaics would only be used when the electricity generated has a high value. Remote telecommunications and navigational beacons are the best examples. Another example would be medical refrigerators if the state is prepared to pay.

For pumping small volumes of water (e.g. village water supply) photovoltaics would typically not be able to compete with manual pumps even with the anticipated price fall of the next decade. At higher levels of water demand (e.g. irrigation of a few hectares) photovoltaics are normally hopelessly uncompetitive with diesel pumps.

It is also suggested that photovoltaic-powered systems are extremely reliable. However, this is usually overstated. Faults do occur in the batteries and electric motors that are fed by the arrays. Breakages can also happen, and dirt on and damage of the array covering reduces output. For example, in a survey of 15 photovoltaic pumps in Pakistan, Howes (1982) reported that 6 were not used owing to technical problems, while in a study of photovoltaic-powered lighting in Fiji, Bhatia (1985) observed that there were problems with nearly half the light fixtures because of their poor quality. Nonetheless, PV systems may be more cost effective than kerosene lamps for lighting.

Windmills

Windmills have been used for centuries to supply shaft power for milling and water pumping. They are currently produced in several countries. The major developing country manufacturers are Argentina and China.

Windmills are conceptually similar to photovoltaics in that quite high capital costs are required, but that the source of energy is free. Clearly the cost of a windmill depends upon the local wind conditions. Bhatia (1984b) has calculated the economics of a windmill for different cropping patterns in northern India. He sized the windmill by calculating a critical month given by the maximum ratio of energy demand (given by the demand for water and the head through which it is lifted) to average windspeed. Under these assumptions Bhatia's cheapest windmill had a capital cost equivalent to a photovoltaic pump of $6.5 per peak Watt.

A problem with using wind as an energy source is that its speed is variable. If the windspeed is too slight the windmill will not start, but if it is too strong the windmill may be damaged. When a guaranteed supply of water is needed in the critical month (e.g. with sensitive high-yielding crops) then the windmill should be sized according to some likely minimum windspeed in that month (at some confidence level), possibly leading to a much larger and more expensive windmill.

An alternative is to pump water into a storage tank at times of good windspeed to maintain the water supply when windspeeds are low. This cannot usually be done for crop irrigation as the volumes of water needed are too large. However, a windmill with a tank can be used for village water supply, and for pumping drinking water for livestock.

Windmills used for water pumping can turn at slow speeds and can be made with relatively low tolerances. For generating electricity much higher speeds are needed, often hundreds of revolutions per minute, and many new designs have been developed, such as vertical windmills.

Windmills for water pumping are usually quite simple mechanical devices, and thus relatively easy to maintain and repair. It is most important that windmills are designed so that they shut down in hurricanes and typhoons. Ward *et al.* (1984) note that this has been a problem in much of Africa.

Water turbines

The use of river flow to power agricultural processing equipment is another form of renewable energy that has been used for centuries. Its applicability is, of course, very site specific.

The modern use of water turbines falls into two main categories: small sizes of around 10 kW which are used to drive mills, grinders, oil expellers, etc; and hydro-electric generators. Turbines in this latter category may have capacities of anything from a few kilowatts to several megawatts.

China is perhaps the best known country where small hydro power is used on a wide scale. Here more than 90,000 turbines had been installed by

1980 (Taylor, 1983). More recently, a water turbine industry has appeared in Nepal, where they are used primarily for agricultural processing (see Sharma, 1988, and Ashworth, 1985).

If the terrain is suitable, water turbines can compete with diesel engines and electric motors for shaft power. We have already noted that in larger sizes they can be part of a decentralized electricity generation system. As with windmills they are relatively simple devices to operate and maintain.

Biogas plants

Biogas plants or digesters convert animal dung (although other fuels can be used) into methane. Digesters have been installed in numerous countries. More have been built in China than elsewhere, where more than seven million biogas plants have been installed. India, a country with some 180 million cattle (Ward *et al.*, 1980, table 3) lags some way behind with about one million biogas plants.

There are two main designs, the Chinese fixed dome variety, and the Indian version with a metal floating dome that rises and falls with the gas volume. However, the Chinese design is also widely used in India. Gas production rates depend upon the size of pit, and on average it takes between 25 and 30 kg of dung to make one cubic metre of gas (see Santerre and Smith, 1982; Barnett *et al.*, 1978, 1990). This is a conversion efficiency of about 40 per cent. An important feature of biogas generation is that the residue slurry has the same fertilizer content as the raw dung, and can be spread on the fields in a similar manner.

The gas can be used for cooking and lighting in the rural household, or to substitute for diesel oil in engines. In this latter case some diesel oil must be used as a supplement, and it is usual to replace 80 per cent of the diesel oil with gas.

A 3.75 kW diesel engine running at half-load for four hours per day would require a gas plant supplying 4.5 cubic metres per day. This would use approximately 120 kg of dung per day, the production of some ten head of adult cattle. Households usually use less gas for cooking and a plant supplying 2 cubic metres per day could be sufficient for one family (with four or more cattle).

Because of the large volume of dung needed, biogas plants normally require cattle to be kept in stalls next to the biogas plant. This means there are two options: have the biogas in the fields where an engine can be used for irrigation, or to have the biogas plant near the house where the gas can be used primarily for cooking. This latter option has been followed in most countries. Unfortunately the economics are not favourable for this application because of the relatively cheap price of wood and subsidized kerosene. Note also the biogas plant is not movable. If the fields operated by a farmer are fragmented a biogas-fuelled engine may be much less suitable than a fully diesel-fuelled one. Diesel pumpsets can be carried from field to field on animal carts (boreholes can be drilled in several locations).

Human faeces could also be used as a feedstock for the biogas plant and this is done in China. It has the advantage of killing pathogens and is a form of waste treatment. As such a biogas plant could be integrated into a programme of village sanitation. However, in India and other countries there are strong taboos against cooking on gas from faeces.

Using a dispersed feedstock such as the dung of grazing cattle or water hyacinth requires large amounts of labour to collect the biomass and carry it to the gas plant. When designing these types of schemes it is common for the supply of such feedstocks to be overestimated, resulting in operational problems.

Successful use of a biogas plant requires an adequate standard of construction. In China the impressive diffusion of biogas plants was achieved by sacrificing quality, and more than half the biogas plants that were built are no longer operational.

Gasifiers

An alternative method of substituting for diesel oil in a diesel engine is to use a gasifier. This involves the partial combustion of wood, other biomass, and charcoal to produce carbon monoxide (with a little hydrogen). Gasifiers were widely used to power vehicles in Europe during fuel shortages in World War II. Today, gasifiers are most widely used in Brazil, where more than 2000 units were sold in 1986. Numerous other countries also have gasifiers installed and operating, including India and Thailand. Usually the diesel engine is fitted with a spark-ignition system, and is fuelled only with gas.

The gasification reaction takes place only at high temperatures, and maintaining the correct flow of fuel requires a skilled operator when the gasifier is running. Efficiencies are high and even a simple gasifier can attain 60 per cent (see FAO, 1986; Foley and Barnard, 1983).

When biomass is used as a fuel, the gas contains tars that will damage an engine. These must be removed with filters. For small engines of less than 10 kW this becomes expensive and technically difficult (i.e. the engine does not produce sufficient suction). In this case charcoal must be used as the fuel: here volatile tars have already been driven off in the charcoal-making process. Most small gasifiers are in the protoype stage rather than being fully developed designs.

When using wood and charcoal, the cost of running a gasifier is sensitive to the local fuelwood situation. In the Philippines, for example, the programme of the Gasifier Equipment Manufacturing Corporation (GEMCOR) was drastically hit by a doubling in the price of charcoal from 1981 to 1984. A survey in May 1984 found that two-thirds of the 242 gasifiers installed by GEMCOR were not operating (Bernardo, 1990).

Gasifiers can also be used to convert boilers to biomass fuels. The gasifier is placed next to the boiler and the gas piped into the boiler. This means that boilers designed to use a liquid of gaseous fuel can be fuelled with a solid biomass fuel. This is particularly suitable for agricultural processing plants that have large quantities of biomass as a by-product (e.g. corn cobs, rice hulls, coconut husks). The handling of these fuels can pose problems, however.

Steam engines

An alternative to a gasifier in some situations may be a steam engine. Small low-pressure steam-reciprocating engines combined with boilers and heat exchangers are very expensive, but they are reliable and relatively easy to maintain. Such engines were widely used in Europe during the last century. More recently, a few engines have been installed successfully in a few locations.

Handpumps and animal-powered pumps

Clearly, one option is to use people or animals as a source of energy. Quite how one categorizes these energy sources is a matter of debate. In general the use of labour and animals is better analysed within an economic framework rather than one that emphasizes energy. However, a specific discussion of handpumps and animal-powered pumps is included as these may substitute for small engine-powered pumps.

Handpumps, or indeed footpumps, are used mainly for pumping drinking water, although they are also used to irrigate small plots in some areas. They come in a wide variety of designs ranging in cost from $50 to $1000. (See World Bank 1987c.) The attractiveness of manual pumping depends upon the opportunity cost of the labour used. It can never be zero, as heavy manual work uses energy and requires the worker to eat more to maintain the same nutritional status. People cannot usually sustain a work-rate above about 50 W. A person working at this rate for one hour would be able to pump about 1 cubic metre of water through a height of 10 metres, enough water for 30 people for one day.

At a subsistence wage of about $1 per day, cheap manual pumps are normally the most cost-effective method of meeting small demands for water. Their use may also be suitable for marginal farmers cropping less than a hectare.

Animal-powered pumps, such as the Persian Wheel, are another traditional method of pumping water. Here an open well (instead of a bore) is required to below the level of the groundwater. This involves digging the well and lining it with bricks, and the result is a much more expensive well. Some animal-powered pumps using a bore have been designed, but all are in the prototype stage (see Hurst, 1985).

Animals also have limits on the work that they can do. A pair of bullocks can produce about 1 kW, and is able to work for about six hours per day. They can pump about 100 cubic metres per day through a 10-metre lift. Animal pumps cannot usually compete with diesel pumps unless an open well happens to be already available, and the animals used have other income-generating activities. Adequate fodder, especially during the dry season, could also be a constraint.

Factors in the choice of technology

Reliability remains an important issue even with renewable energy technologies. With renewable energy technologies the reliability of the energy source, wind for windmills, river flow for water turbines, sunshine for photovoltaics, animal dung for biogas plants, may be high. The overall reliability in performing whatever task is needed depends then upon the technology installed. In addition to the inherent quality of the device, the ability to keep it running depends upon ready access to skilled maintenance and spare parts.

Effective local participation is essential. Because renewable energy technologies often have higher capital costs (but lower operating costs) than more conventional petroleum engines and electric motors, they are often proposed for community projects. This reduces the capital investment per consumer and makes renewable technologies more competitive. As with community forestry projects, success depends upon the co-operation of all members of the community (see Lichtman, 1987, for a discussion of the problems with community biogas plants). This implies some organization for managing the project, to distribute its benefits and costs in a way that does not threaten any sub-group.

No particular technology can be proposed without careful analysis

Little can be said about the choice of technology in general. Most renewable energy technologies substitute a recurrent cost (i.e. the annual fuel bill) for an initial capital investment. If diesel oil or electricity are subsidized, this lessens the financial attractiveness of renewable technologies and consequently makes them harder to disseminate.

Almost every technology will be optimal in some location for some particular task (for an economic analysis of some options see Bhatia, 1984b, 1987; Hurst, 1985, 1988). As a consequence, a detailed analysis of each location is needed. Advocating one type of technology, particularly untried and experimental devices, is almost certainly going to be very risky and imprudent. However, petroleum products and rural electrification will be the primary methods of supplying modern energy in most locations.

The choice of energy intervention will depend upon local resources, the capability of rural institutions, and most importantly the requirements and needs of local people.

As discussed in Chapters 1 and 2, the collection of information on rural conditions, and the assessment of policy alternatives, are often hampered by the vertical hierarchies of the relevant government ministries (e.g. Agriculture, Energy, Forestry, etc). Special attention must be given to institutional methods of bridging the gap between these different agencies for successful rural energy projects.

Rural energy projects are often small and site specific. This makes projects difficult to plan and implement. However, many small but effective energy projects, co-ordinated with other rural projects, can lead to real and sustainable development.

Annexes

Annexe I: check-lists for rural projects

This Annexe supplements the administrative actions suggested in Chapter 2 and provides a check-list of energy issues that administrators and project designers should consider in rural development projects. As many issues are common to all projects, we start with four general propositions.

General check-list

1. Is the current state of the chosen energy supply sufficient for the project?

Many projects have *direct* energy demands, i.e. they incorporate activities that require energy of some type. For example:

○ rural transportation projects that introduce mechanized road vehicles require petroleum products;

○ tractors and power tillers need diesel oil;

○ pumps for irrigation and agricultural processing equipment require a power source;

○ pumps for village water supply need a power source as do pumps for livestock projects;

○ electricity may be needed for rural telecommunications; refrigerators for rural health centres, lathes and other tools in rural workshops, and refrigerators to freeze fish, meat and milk in livestock processing plants;

○ many rural industries require heat and may need wood;

○ many rural industries also require a power source.

Main issues

The existing energy supply may be inadequate for the new demands created by rural development. Further, new investments in energy supply may allow a different range of options to be considered and so improve the profitability of the project.

In addition to technical solutions such as stringing new electricity lines, introducing new energy technologies, or planting woodland with new tree species, it is important that the general policy environment, including pricing policies and the development of local institutions, is analysed for suitable interventions.

In calculating project economics it should be noted that the costs of distributing petroleum products to rural areas are often high (the rural price may be more than double the border price), and that there are often economies of scale to energy investments. Project planners and consultants must analyse the effect of investments in energy on the project economics. Many energy projects will have the primary role to guarantee the security of energy supply rather than to increase average consumption dramatically. Hence they improve the economics of a project from a very low rate of return (when an energy shortage occurs) to an acceptable level.

Actions

- O Analyse the current energy situation. Is the supply of energy sufficient at all times of the year?

- O Check the changes in the rate of return of the proposed project to probable and possible shortfalls in energy. Are the project economics sensitive to energy supply?

- O Consider additional investment to reinforce the supply of existing fuels. This may mean investment in the infrastructure used to distribute diesel oil, and in rural electrification.

- O Consider new energy supplies not currently in use (e.g. rural electrification in area where it is not currently used, renewable energy technologies, etc). Do these improve the rate of return of the project?

2. Does the project lead to other — indirect — demands for energy?

Some projects have *indirect* energy demands. Of course, these are harder to identify than direct energy demands, but may be no less crucial for the success of a development project. These energy demands occur because an intervention in one sector results in the demand for another energy-consuming activity. While the need for these complementary activities is often understood, these secondary demands for energy often do not receive sufficient attention. For example:

- O any agricultural development programme will increase the energy demands of rural industries that process agricultural produce;

- O any agricultural development programme will increase the demand for energy used for rural transportation;

- O projects that will increase the demand for energy for the preparation

91

of food in the rural household include resettlement, agricultural development, food security, and food aid;

○ irrigation, road, and rural sanitation projects that require bricks will increase the demand for wood by rural brickworks;

○ fishery projects may increase the demand for wood for fish smoking.

Main issues

Some of these indirect energy demands are far from obvious. For example, anyone planning the resettlement of a group of people has to consider many aspects of rural life to ensure that the new settlement will be viable. It is very easy to overlook the fact that wood will be needed if food is to be cooked. The people moved to a new location will simply move on again if they cannot find sufficient fuel.

Indirect demands for energy may be quite different in nature from the direct energy demands of the project. This is most clearly the case where modern forms of energy are used to increase agricultural productivity, but where traditional forms of energy are used in crop processing. This occurs with tobacco curing and tea drying, for example. A similar situation could exist where crops are irrigated with diesel pumpsets, but where processing industries are equipped with electric motors. Even if a reliable supply of diesel oil is available, it does not follow that there can be the same level of confidence in the electricity supply.

Using the same type of energy for both direct and indirect energy demands (where applicable) has the advantage of economies of scale in capital expenditure and administrative overheads.

Using different energy sources has the attraction of diversifying energy supply which may increase the overall project reliability.

Actions

○ Identify associated activities needed for the success of a particular project, and hence the indirect demands for energy.

○ Consider the range of supply options needed to meet these energy demands, and plan the necessary energy support project. Pay particular attention to complementary activities that require wood, as deforestation is a problem in many areas.

○ The actions for direct energy demand analysis also apply here.

3. Does the project have complementary energy projects in addition to any direct or indirect energy demands?

A rural development project may also have an energy component that although not meeting any direct or indirect energy demand nonetheless enhances the project and has an overall development impact. Indeed, it is possible for there to be energy solutions to non-energy problems.

For example:

○ trees can be planted around irrigation canals, barrages and dams — in addition to providing a future source of woodfuel, this helps reduce siltation;

○ trees can be planted around hydro-electric schemes;

○ fuelwood projects can have saleable by-products such as fodder, poles and fruit which can be incorporated into agricultural development projects;

○ tree planting is, of course, a component of environmental projects designed to reduce deforestation and desertification — a fuelwood component can also be planned;

○ programmes to improve the status of women should also consider tree planting as a method of reducing the time needed for fuel collection;

○ the pumping of a village water supply can release women's time for more fruitful activities;

○ improved stove projects (both rural and urban) can be associated with women's projects.

Main issues

The range of energy projects that can be associated with a rural development project is large, the difficulty being to identify those that can have a significant development impact. It will often be the case that tree planting will be desirable.

A new supply of energy can also permit other development activities to take place that would otherwise be impossible (e.g. an electricity supply for a village water project can be made to service medical centres and schools).

Actions

○ The planting and management of trees should be considered as part of the majority of projects. This is often justified by the economic benefits of an enhanced supply of fuelwood and other products, and by long-term environmental benefits.

○ Nearly all projects should analyse both the rural petroleum product market and the potential for rural electrification. Investments in one of these options will almost always have important benefits. However, other complementary investments in end-use equipment must not be forgotten.

○ Alternative methods of introducing modern forms of energy (e.g. renewable energy technologies) should be considered if a source of shaft power or electricity is needed.

4. Are non-technical solutions possible to energy-related problems?

Just as energy projects can help to alleviate non-energy problems, the reverse also holds. It is easy to confuse energy interventions with the introduction of new hardware, but this need not be so. As discussed at length in Chapter 3, many of the rural energy problems are the result of the social, political and economic organization of rural life. Adjusting the rural policy environment can have a major effect on energy supply and demand.

For example:

○ rural development projects may be designed so as to reduce need for energy supplies (through low tillage systems, different cropping patterns and so on);

○ increasing the controlled price of agricultural produce will lead to an increase in income to buy energy and this in turn will increase the demand for energy;

○ increasing the controlled price of energy products may encourage private investment in decentralized energy supply;

○ the provision of credit institutions may allow consumers to buy the necessary equipment to consume energy more efficiently;

○ the development of local institutions may permit community projects such as village woodland;

○ the training of mechanics can help to make energy equipment more reliable.

Main issues

Energy prices in rural areas are often highly distorted. This can dramatically affect the attractiveness of investing in energy supply.

Energy will only be consumed if suitable appliances can be purchased by consumers and can be kept operating.

The economics of energy projects are very site specific. Local resource assessments are required.

The different groups within rural society often have conflicting objectives. This must be taken into account in project design.

Option matrix

ANNEXE I:
RURAL DEVELOPMENT PROJECT/PROGRAMMES

Main energy options to consider

TYPE OF PROJECT

	Farming/mechanization	Livestock	Fishery	Irrigation	Rural industries	Women	Village water supply/sanitation	Rural health	Tourism	Telecommunications	Desertification	Resettlement/food aid	Transportation	Page No.
PETROLEUM PRODUCT DISTRIBUTION														
Availability/Reliability	*	*	*	*	*	*	*	*	*	*	*	*	*	
Emergency back-up equipment and storage	*	*	*	*			*	*	*	*		*		
Using equipment efficiency	*	*	*	*	*					*		*		145
LOCAL ELECTRICITY GRID														
Connection to the main grid	*	*	*	*	*	*	*	*	*	*	*		*	109
Diesel generator	*	*	*	*	*	*	*	*	*	*	*		*	110
Biomass conversion	*			*										110
Hydro-plants	*		*	*						*				110, 132
Aerogenerators		*					*	*		*				110, 140
Photovoltaic plants				*			*	*		*				110, 134
VILLAGE PRE-ELECTRIFICATION						*	*	*	*	*		*		108
HEAT/SHAFT PRODUCTION BY RET														
Gasifiers		*		*								*		128
Boilers	*			*										126
Biogas		*					*							130
Water turbines	*		*	*										132
Windmills	*	*		*			*			*				117, 134
Solar driers	*	*	*											138
Solar water heaters							*	*	*					137
Hand/foot pumps						*	*	*			*			114
Animal powered pumps	*	*		*			*			*				116
Photovoltaic pumps						*	*	*	*		*			119
Using equipment efficiency	*	*	*	*	*		*	*		*				
COLD PRODUCTION														
PV fridge/deep freezer						*		*	*					147
WOODFUEL INTERVENTIONS														
Forestry programmes	*	*				*				*	*			
Specific/private woodland		*		*	*		*	*		*	*			
Complementary plantations	*	*	*	*	*		*			*	*	*		
Using equipment efficiency	*	*					*	*	*					
Charcoal kiln efficiency	*	*		*						*				124
Woodstove programmes	*					*		*		*	*			143, 144
COMMUNITY ORGANIZATION						*	*	*	*		*	*	*	
MACRO-POLICY RECOMMENDATIONS														
Pricing policy	*	*	*	*	*	*				*				
Rural credit policy	*	*	*	*	*	*	*	*		*	*	*	*	

95

Actions

○ Any proposed energy project should analyse pricing policy and rural credit institutions.

○ Any proposed energy project must include a component of staff planning and vocational training.

○ Any community-level project must analyse social structures within the target areas.

Check-lists for specific types of project

The items listed for each sector cannot cover every eventuality and provide an indication of the energy impact analysis that should be incorporated into the documentation of proposed projects. The chart on page 95 shows the technical options that could commonly be considered with each type of rural development project.

PROJECT TYPE 1

AGRICULTURAL DEVELOPMENT

Farming systems and mechanization

What is the state of the energy source or the efficiency of equipment to be used for the new systems?

○ irrigation pumps;

○ tractors and tillers;

○ threshers, grinders, etc;

○ other on-farm crop processing (drying, boiling, etc);

○ rural industries processing crop output;

○ transportation of produce from fields to market centres and rural industries;

○ transportation from rural industries to urban areas;

○ repairing farm equipment.

What impact will there be on the rural woodfuel supply from the planned changes of cropping pattern?

○ the expansion of agricultural land over woodland;

○ the transfer of fallow land to cropped land;

- changes in crop by-products (i.e. the suitability of agricultural residues as a fuel);
- changes in access to land by landless labourers;
- increase demand for woodfuel by rural industries.

Consider

- investments in the supply and storage of petroleum products;
- investments in engine maintenance and related training;
- investments in rural electrification (both grid and decentralized);
- water turbines for crop processing if suitable river flow is available;
- solar driers;
- gasifiers for process heat;
- pricing policies;
- forestry (trees can provide fruit and poles);
- improved stove programmes (both rural and urban).

Livestock

What is the state of the energy source or the efficiency of equipment to be used for the new procedures?

- pumping drinking water;
- processing milk and meat;
- refrigeration of animal products;
- transporting animal products to market places?

What impact will there be on the rural woodfuel supply from the additional animals?

- a change in land-use patterns;
- the destruction of small trees from grazing on fallow land and roadsides;
- the loss of dung as a fuel for landless people if cattle are kept in sheds.

Consider

- investments in the supply of petroleum products;

- ○ investments in rural electrification (both grid and decentralized);
- ○ biogas plants if animals are kept in sheds;
- ○ windmills for pumping drinking water;
- ○ pricing policies;
- ○ forestry programmes (trees can provide fodder).

Fishery

What is the state of the energy source or the efficiency of equipment to be used for the projects?

- ○ fishing boats;
- ○ fish treatment plants and storage of produce (e.g. refrigeration and drying);
- ○ fish smoking;
- ○ transportation of fish to markets;
- ○ repairing boats.

What impact will there be on the rural woodfuel supply from fishery?

- ○ the burning of wood during fish smoking.

Consider

- ○ investments in the supply of petroleum products;
- ○ investments in rural electrification (both grid and decentralized);
- ○ solar driers;
- ○ improving the efficiency of cooling and freezing;
- ○ woodland specifically for fish smoking;
- ○ improving the efficiency of wood use;
- ○ gasifiers for large firms;
- ○ pricing policies.

Irrigation

What is the state of the energy source or the efficiency of equipment to be used for irrigation?

- ○ running irrigation pumps;

- ○ dredging canals;

- ○ processing increased crop yields including running threshers, grinders, etc;

- ○ other on-farm crop processing of increased yields (drying, boiling, etc);

- ○ rural industries processing crop output;

- ○ transportation of agricultural produce from fields to market centres and rural industries;

- ○ transportation from rural industries to urban areas;

- ○ repairing pumps.

What impact will there be on the rural woodfuel supply from the change of cropping pattern?

- ○ loss of land to civil works;

- ○ the expansion of agricultural land over wood-producing areas;

- ○ the transfer of fallow land to cropped land;

- ○ changes in crop by-products (i.e. the suitability of agricultural wastes as a fuel);

- ○ changes in access to land by landless labourers;

- ○ increase demand for woodfuel by rural industries (including brickworks).

Consider

- ○ investments in the supply of petroleum products;

- ○ investments in rural electrification (both grid and decentralized);

- ○ energy for rural industries (see below);

- ○ pricing policies;

- ○ planting trees around civil works and other forestry projects.

PROJECT TYPE 2

RURAL INDUSTRIES

What is the state of the energy source or the efficiency of equipment to be used for rural industries?

- heat for the processing of agricultural produce (e.g. tea drying, sugar production, etc);
- shaft power for the processing of agricultural produce (e.g. rice mills, cotton gins, etc);
- shaft power for lumber mills and plywood factories;
- rural workshops;
- other rural industries (e.g. textiles).

What impact will there be on the rural woodfuel supply from an increase in rural industrial activity?

- charcoal manufacture;
- brickmaking;
- drying of agricultural produce.

Consider

- investments in the supply of petroleum products;
- investments in rural electrification (both grid and decentralized)
- water turbines for crop processing if suitable river flow is available;
- solar driers;
- woodland specifically for rural industries;
- gasifiers for larger firms;
- distribution for timber waste for fuel;
- energy conservation by changing production methods;
- pricing policies.

PROJECT TYPE 3

WOMEN'S PROJECTS

What is the state of the energy source or the efficiency of equipment for domestic use?

- cooking;
- domestic lighting;
- water supply.

What impact does the rural woodfuel supply have on the viability of women's projects?

- a large amount of time must be spent cooking and collecting fuel;

- inferior smoky fuels cause respiratory problems;

- diets change adversely if the supply is inadequate.

Consider

- investments in the supply of petroleum products;

- investments in rural electrification (both grid and decentralized);

- rural and urban stove programmes;

- forestry programmes;

- introducing a village water supply (see below).

PROJECT TYPE 4

VILLAGE WATER SUPPLY AND SANITATION

What is the state of the energy source or the efficiency of equipment to be used?

- water pumps;

- workshops to maintain and repair manual pumps.

Consider

- investments in the supply of petroleum products;

- investments in rural electrification (both grid and decentralized);

- windmills;

- handpumps;

- community organization;

- biogas plants supplied by latrines.

PROJECT TYPE 5

RURAL HEALTH

What is the state of the energy source or the efficiency of equipment to be used for

- medical refrigerators;

- ○ sterilization;
- ○ heating water;
- ○ lighting.

Consider

- ○ investments in the supply of petroleum products;
- ○ investments in rural electrification (both grid and decentralized);
- ○ photovoltaic arrays;
- ○ wind-electric generators;
- ○ solar water heaters;
- ○ planting woodland to service health centres.

PROJECT TYPE 6

TOURISM

What is the state of the energy source or the efficiency of equipment to be used for

- ○ water heating;
- ○ cooking;
- ○ air conditioning;
- ○ lighting;
- ○ transport and communications.

What impact will hotel development projects in rural areas have on the rural woodfuel supply?

- ○ the migration of the hotel workers and their families;
- ○ the migration of people to live and work along roads built to service hotels.

Consider

- ○ investments in the supply of petroleum products;
- ○ investments in rural electrification (both grid and decentralized);
- ○ the necessity for back-up energy sources to provide adequate reliability;

- ○ solar water heaters;
- ○ planting trees around hotels in rural areas and along supply roads.

PROJECT TYPE 7

TELECOMMUNICATIONS

What is the state of the energy source or the efficiency of equipment to be used for

- ○ powering radio repeaters;
- ○ navigational beacons;
- ○ other telecommunication equipment.

Consider

- ○ investments in the supply of petroleum products;
- ○ investments in rural electrification (both grid and decentralized);
- ○ photovoltaic arrays;
- ○ wind-electric generators.

PROJECT TYPE 8

DESERTIFICATION AND DEFORESTATION CONTROL

What is the state of the energy source or the efficiency of equipment to be used for

- ○ land preparation;
- ○ irrigation and mechanized silviculture.

What is the relationship between deforestation and the loss of wood resulting from

- ○ consumption by households in rural areas;
- ○ consumption by households in urbal areas;
- ○ consumption by rural and urban industries;
- ○ charcoal production;
- ○ changes in land-use patterns.

Consider

- ○ investments in the supply of petroleum products;

- ○ investments in rural electrification (both grid and decentralized)
- ○ social forestry and private tree growing;
- ○ stove programmes;
- ○ decreasing the wood consumption of rural industries;
- ○ pricing policies.

PROJECT TYPE 9

RESETTLEMENT AND FOOD AID

What is the state of the energy source or the efficiency of equipment to be used for

- ○ transporting goods and people;
- ○ cooking;
- ○ food storage.

What impact will the effects of migration of rural populations have on the rural woodfuel supply from

- ○ domestic needs for wood.

Consider

- ○ emergency supplies of petroleum products;
- ○ forestry programmes for permanent resettlement.

PROJECT TYPE 10

TRANSPORTATION

What is the state of the energy source or the efficiency of equipment to be used for

- ○ mechanized vehicles;
- ○ repair workshops;
- ○ navigational beacons for boats.

Consider

- ○ investments in the supply of petroleum products;
- ○ investments in rural electrification (both grid and decentralized);
- ○ photovoltaic-powered buoys;

- energy impacts of the development of different transport modes;
- energy impact of the development of different distribution, storage, retail and design options.

PROJECT TYPE 11

EDUCATION

What is the state of the energy source or the efficiency of equipment to be used for

- lighting;
- cooking;
- communications;
- school workshops or the school farm.

Consider

- photovoltaic lighting;
- fuelwood planting;
- institutional-sized woodstove and boiler;
- biogas for cooking and lighting;
- diesel generators with diesel storage facilities.

Annexe II: Fact sheets for rural energy supply options

Contacts and references

Where to get additional information

While local experience must be drawn upon in any project, experience with technologies elsewhere is a useful starting point when considering technologies for rural development. The data given in these fact sheets are only illustrative, and actual costs and technical characteristics will vary from site to site.

References and contacts

While many institutions have worked with energy supply issues for years, the organizations listed below provide a good sample of those that can provide information on the application of energy technologies in rural areas.

ACES Arab Centre for Energy Studies, PO Box 20501, Safat, Kuwait.

AIT Asian Institute of Technology: Energy Technology Division, PO Box 2754, Bangkok, Thailand.

ASTRA Indian Institute of Science, Bangalore 560012, India.

CATAMI Centre d'Accueil des Technologies Avancées et de la Maîtrise Industrielle, BP 1239, Antananarivo 101, Madagascar.

ENDA-TM Environnement et Développement du Tiers-Monde, BP 3370, Dakar, Sénégal.

ENERCAL Société Néo-calédonienne d'Energie, BP C1, Nouméa Cedex, Nouvelle-Calédonie.

IAT Institute of Appropriate Technology, Bangladesh University of Engineering & Technology, Dhaka 2, Bangladesh.

ITESA/INET Institute of Nuclear Energy Technology, Tsingua Univesity, PO Box 1021, Beijing, China.

OLADE Casilla 6413 CCI, Quito, Ecuador.

TERI Tata Energy Research Institute, 7 Jor Bagh, New Delhi 110003, India.

UN PEDP Pacific Energy Development Programme, 11 Desvoeux Road, Private Bag, Suva, Fiji.

SCAFEDES Association Française pour l'Etude et le Développement des Applications de l'Energie Solaire, 28 rue de la Source, 75016 Paris, France.

AFME Agence Français pour la Maîtrise de l'Energie, 27 rue Louis-Vicat, 75737 Paris, France.

ATI Appropriate Technology International, 1331 H Street NW, Washington DC, 20005, USA.

Aqua Viva, Fondation Sahel Aqua Viva, 4 rue Saint-Saëns, 75015 Paris, France.

BRI Brace Research Institute, MacDonald College of McGill University, 1 Stewart Park, Ste. Anne de Bellevue, Quebec, Canada.

CEC Commission of the European Community, DGVIII, rue de la Loi 200, B-1049 Brussels, Belgium.

CEEMAT Centre d'Etude et d'Expérimentation du Machinisme Agricole Tropical, Parc du Tourvoie, 92160 Antony, France.

CIRED Centre International de Recherche sur l'Environnement et le Développement, 10 rue Monsieur le Prince, 75005 Paris, France.

Club du Sahel, 2 rue André Pascal, 75775 Paris Cedex 16, France.

CTFT Centre Technique Forestier Tropical, 45 bis avenue de la Belle Gabrielle, 94736 Nogent-sur-Marne, France.

GERES Groupe Energie Renouvelables, 73 avenue Corot, 13013 Marseille, France.

GESTE Groupe d'Echanges Scientifiques et Techniques, 2 rue Antoine Etex, Immeuble 'les Gémeaux', 94000 Creteil, France.

GRET Groupe de Recherche et d'Echanges Technologiques: Cellule Energies Renouvelables, 213 rue Lafayette, 75010 Paris, France.

IDRC International Development Research Centre, PO Box 8500, Ottawa, Canada.

ITD Institut Technologique DELLO, Le Moulin Rouge, 60410 Verberie, France.

ITDG Intermediate Technology Development Group, Myson House, Railway Terrace, Rugby, CV21 3HT, UK.

ORSTOM Office de la Recherche Scientifique et Technique Outre-Mer, 24 rue Bayard, 75008 Paris, France.

TWENTE Technology & Development Group, Twente University of Technology, PO Box 217, 7500 AE Enschede, The Netherlands.

VITA Volunteers in Technical Assistance, 80 S Early Street, Alexandria, Virginia 22304, USA.

RURAL ELECTRIFICATION

Rural electrification by grid extension

Description

Extensions of bulk supply grid to provide electricity (single or three-phase, 110 or 240 volts, 50 or 60Hz), generally are:

- ○ incremental extension to areas that are close to bulk supply grids and which currently obtain power from isolated generators;

- ○ replacements to stand-alone generation;

- ○ additions to existing generation.

Transmission/distribution technology is mature (though still undergoing incremental improvement). Lower cost single wire earth return (SWER) systems are being adopted in some countries (Australia, Argentina).

Extent of use and demand

There is considerable variation within and between countries: electrification by grid is highest in Latin America followed by Asia (around 30 per cent in China and 25 per cent in India) then Africa (less than 10 per cent). Note that the number of households using electricity may be lower than the number of households connected.

Rural electricity is principally used for domestic lighting and shaft power applications in irrigation and industry.

Constraints and costs

Capital costs are dominated by the transmission component and thus increase rapidly with distance from bulk supply system. Considerable skill is required to install, operate and maintain electricity transmission and sub-station equipment (little skill is required to install and maintain wooden poles). Medium skills are required to install and maintain distribution network.

Transmission and distribution transformers have a long lifetime (around 20 years). However there may be long delays in repairing breakdowns.

Low load factors and long distances mean high losses in transmission and distribution (about 20 per cent excluding theft). The average connection cost for a new subscriber is estimated at $3,000 in Zaire and $6,000 in Paraguay, medium voltage transmission lines: $7,500–$50,000 per km (*Guide de l'Energie*, 1987).

Impact on rural development and perspectives

Grid electricity is a clean (at point of use) and versatile source of energy. It can stimulate commercial and industrial activities by providing a lower energy cost to users for electrically powered appliances.

However, its role as a catalyst for rural development is almost certainly dependent on complementary inputs. Since there are high connection charges and appliance costs, any benefits usually accrue to wealthier households. Supply may be unreliable (as a result of power cuts and voltage reductions) and is outside the control of the user.

Autonomous production of electricity

Local production tends to be adopted when the connection to the grid is not possible. This solution presents two constraints in addition to problems associated with grid electricity:

○ local availability of the primary energy resource;

○ local capacities for permanent operation, maintenance and management.

Diesel generators (see also p. 145)

Considered by national utilities as the best solution for remote areas (because of transmission losses of the national grid) and with installed capacities of 50–500 kW, more and more diesel plants are being run by cooperatives. The main characteristics are:

○ low capital costs: long lifetimes (10,000–40,000 hours depending on the maintenance quality), but high operating costs (20–80 per cent of the total cost of kWh depending on size and loading rate);

○ difficulties and cost of diesel oil supply;

○ permanent staff of qualified technicians to meet a low demand;

○ difficulties in bill payment collection.

Mini-hydro plants (see also p. 132)

Mini-hydro is often considered the most economically viable solution (high capital costs but mature and reliable technology) where there is a water supply, and the following conditions are satisfied:

○ high level of use, high load factor, no rapid load variations;

○ high water head, regular flow, no complex civil engineering required;

○ user equipment close to the generator (less than 10 km).

Biomass conversion (see also pp. 126–131)

This is considered a flexible solution where wood or other biomass products are abundant. Shaft power for alternators can be provided using conversion processes such as:

○ boilers with steam turbines – generally for plants greater than 1MW, fed with wood (as in Philippines or Brazil) or biomass residues (from the sugar industry).

○ gasifiers with diesel engines for under 1MW (but commercially available for capacities much less than 100 kW and only for a few biomass products).

○ biogas digesters with diesel engines are operational in some specific contexts (some agro-industries, effluent disposal plants).

Aerogenerators (see also p. 140)

Aerogenerators are suitable only for windspeeds greater than 6m/s and when connected to a main grid (wind farms). Very high capital costs, and requires pilot projects to establish economic viability.

Photovoltaic plants (see also p. 134)

Photovoltaic plants require complex technology (invertors to change from DC to AC) and batteries for storage (often the weak point of the system). Most viable for pre-electrification.

Rural pre-electrification

The concept of rural pre-electrification

Many rural electrification programmes have failed for a wide range of different reasons (see constraints related to national or local grids, p. 108).
Basic needs of rural populations, requiring very small quantities of electricity, can sometimes be met through small-scale generation systems. Such small supplies of energy can change the livelihood of rural populations and prepare them for a future larger scale electrification (when the demand becomes more significant).

Basic needs

Costs will have to be met by government (as part of the general infrastructure) as they frequently exceed users' ability to pay.
Basic and priority activities require some hundreds of Watt-hours/day; for example:

110

- 100 Wh/day for schools (lighting and radio/television);
- 300 Wh/day for health centre (lighting and refrigeration);
- 200 Wh/day for social work (lighting and audio-visual aids);
- 100 Wh/day for community television set;
- 100 Wh/day for telecommunications;
- 50–70 Wh/day per household (lighting and radio/television).

Pre-electrification programmes

Pre-electrification programmes are aimed at preparing consumers for future networks. Their economic viability usually requires:

- real demand from co-operatives or households (costs of the new service should be no more than the cost of traditional equipment: candles, kerosene lamps);
- a credit system enabling them to buy appliances;
- a robust and optimal technical solution.

Trial programmes of this type have been implemented in some countries e.g. Morocco.

Technical solutions

Electricity generation

Depending on the local situation and resources:

- small diesel or gasoline generators (see p. 145);
- photovoltaic generators (see p. 134);
- small aerogenerators (see p. 140);
- mini-/micro-hydro plants (see p. 132) etc.

Distribution

Transport of electricity over short distances can be through low voltage lines (if there are enough users) or batteries recharged (exchanged) in *electricity fountains*. Organizations of this type already exist in some developing countries using car batteries (Maghreb, Asia, Latin America, etc) often in an informal way.

Appliances

High efficiency applicances are already available and could be manufactured locally: fluorescent lights, 20W television sets, highly insulated re-frigerators and deep-freezers, etc. (see also p. 147.)

WATER-PUMPING SYSTEMS

Classification

A. Irrigation

Pumping equipment is required in many irrigation systems. The type and size of the pumping equipment depends on:

○ the agricultural system and its water needs;

○ the water resource and irrigation system (centralized versus decentralized);

○ the local availability and reliability of the energy supply;

○ the local capabilities for operation and maintenance.

Traditional pumps are still common:

○ animal-powered pumps are often used to lift water from heights of 1 to 10 metres (5 to 50 m³ per hour);

○ human-powered pumps are less common for irrigation, but have been used on a large scale in the past.

Pumping systems powered by modern technologies:

○ portable diesel engines with centrifugal pumps (5 to 20hp) adapted for irrigated areas of a few to 30 hectares and a depth up to 10 metres;

○ fixed diesel pumping plants (up to more than 1000hp) often covering hundreds of hectares (centralized irrigation systems).

○ electric pumps connected to the grid, common in Asia, less in Africa.

B. Pumping systems for village water supply

Water requirements generally include:

○ drinking water and other needs for villagers;

○ drinking water for domestic animals;

○ water needs for vegetable plots around households.

Standards adopted varies from 5 litres (basic survival) up to 50 litres (minimum for development) per day per capita.

112

WATER SUPPLY SYSTEM	OUTPUT/HEAD	SUITABLE CONDITIONS	OBSERVATIONS/ COMPARISONS
Traditional well*	5–15m³/day	Existing wells. Suitable ground. Available lining and cover	Check water quality. Traditional use pattern. Cleaning requirements. Very low initial cost
Hand/footpumps (p. 114)	5–10m³/day 10–50m	Remote, isolated, small villages. Low technical capacities	Moderate costs. Good acceptability. Labour requirements for operation and supervision
Animal-powered pumps (p. 116)	10–20m³/day 5–50m	Availability of animals. Low technical environment	Moderate cost. Good acceptability. Costs related to animals. Easy to use
Windmills (p. 117)	10–50m³/day 10–100m	Windspeed >3m/s. Medium villages. Medium technical skill availability	Moderate initial costs. Mature technology. Easy to use. Regular but simple maintenance
Photovoltaic pumps (p. 119)	5–500m³/day 10–100m	High insolation. Large villages. High water needs. Technical skills	Sophisticated technology. High capital costs. Reliability. Low recurrent costs
Aerogenerator pumps (p. 140)	50–100m³/day	Windspeed >5m/s. Isolated sites. High technical skills available	Sophisticated technology. High capital costs. High maintenance costs. Technical qualifications
Diesel pumps (p. 145)	All sizes	Reliable supply of diesel-oil, spare parts, etc. Local skills	Medium capital costs. High recurrent costs. Supervision and maintenance requirements
Electric pumps (grid connected)	All sizes	Possible connection to grid (rare in most parts of Africa)	Low capital cost. Low recurrent cost. Cost of breakdowns in supply. Reliable technology

* In general dug wells (as opposed to boreholes) are not made today, as they are too expensive.

113

The type of pump depends on:

○ the type of the well (traditional or modern) or borehole, and the depth of water table;

○ the local availability and reliability of energy resources;

○ the local capabilities for operation and maintenance.

Pumping systems can:

○ depend on the supply of energy from outside: diesel pump, diesel generator/electric pump, electric pump connected to the grid;

○ be autonomous: hand/foot pumps, animal powered pumps, windmills, solar photovoltaic powered electric pumps, aerogenerator/electric pump.

A combination of several pumping systems may need to be adopted for reasons of supply security.

Handpumps and footpumps

State of the technology

General description

○ Low lift applications, two types: suction (up to 7m) and direct action (up to 12m).

○ Medium/high lift applications, three types: deepwell reciprocating (up to 40m), diaphragm, and progressing cavity.

State of maturity and commercialization

○ Highly mature technology but undergoing development to fit into local environments.

○ Pump reliability (number of breakdowns per year and time taken to make repair) is very important.

Note: the pump is only part of the system; poor well or borehole construction can also cause pump failure.

○ Many hand/footpumps now commercialized with output around 3 to 5m^3 per day (e.g. water needs of 250 villagers) at 20m head.

114

- Many institutes and non-governmental organizations deliver design information and sometimes provide training for construction by local artisans.

- Commercial manufacture possible.

Use in rural areas

State of diffusion in developing countries

- Most economic for low/medium lift (typically <25m) supplies for domestic use especially in areas with poor infrastructure.

- Widespread use (over one million handpumps in India alone). Suction pumps most common type used.

- Local manufacture in many developing countries.

- Installed on more than 90 per cent of the boreholes in West Africa.

Local conditions for use

- Low skills required to operate. Medium skills required to install.

- Generally, village level operation and maintenance (VLOM) requirements met for pumps lifting water less than 25m.

- Villagers have to be prepared to pay for recurrent costs (maintenance).

- May not be used due to loss of social interaction associated with traditional water collection practices.

- Appropriate designs have to be selected (reliability/durability, availability of spare parts).

- Limited to 50m head maximum and 10m^3 per day.

Investment and recurrent costs

- Wells with handpumps estimated to have capital cost $10–30 (1987) per capita. Note: total cost may be dominated by well construction.

- Capital cost in Thailand (1987) for 20 households: $540 for shallow dug well with handpump, and $2,660 for drilled well with handpump.

Advantages

- Relatively simple designs (can be designed for village operation and maintenance). Potential time/energy savings in water collection (for women and children) and positive contribution to health.

○ Handpumps are a lower cost option (no fuel costs) than motor (or engine) driven pumps for the provision of water for non agricultrual purposes.

Disadvantages

○ Low output and generally not applicable for supplies with a lift >40m.

○ Possible adverse health impact if water supply contaminated.

Animal-powered pumps

State of the technology

General description

○ Water pumping using animal (generally bullock) power.

○ Three main types of water lifting equipment:

— *Delou* (rope/pulley and leather bag, 1 bullock): 20m depth, 25m^3/day

— Rope and bucket (2 bullocks): 10m depth, 80m^3/day

— Persian wheel (2 bullocks): 8m depth, 100m^3/day

○ Efficiency of all around 50–65 per cent.

○ Capacity and outputs are above those for hand/footpumps, but below those of motor driven pumps. For example, the *Gueroult* system (with a pair of bullocks) can deliver the same output as 10 to 15 persons (3m^3/hour at 50m head).

○ Needs a dug well (rather than borehole) which may be very expensive to construct if one does not already exist.

State of maturity and commercialization

○ Mature technology.

○ Although industrial production of equipment has been reduced in most industrialized countries, some still used on a large scale (Poland, Spain, etc).

State of transferability

○ Many local organizations and institutes are working on designs appropriate to local conditions and resources.

116

○ Where industrial equipment can be disseminated, no major problem for transfer and local manufacture.

Use in rural areas

State of diffusion in developing countries

○ Found in many parts of Asia.

○ Irrigation in remote locations without access to diesel/electric pumpsets and fuel.

Local conditions for use

○ Adapted to areas where animals are available.

○ Medium skills required to install, operate and maintain.

○ Usually requires existing dug well.

Investment and recurrent costs

○ Capital costs for equipment depend on the design: low for artisanal and locally manufactured systems, high for imported industrial equipment.

○ Recurrent costs linked to cost of animals.

Comparison with other solutions

○ Low capital cost but low output and relatively high cost of animals.

Windmills

State of the technology

General description

○ Wind powered water lifting (shaft power) for provision of irrigation or drinking water (note differences in nature of demand/operation depending on whether use is for drinking or irrigation water).

○ Mechanically driven windmills generally slow running, high mass and high starting torque (start at 3-4m/s windspeed and stop when >10–12m/s).

○ Water storage essential for drinking water applications to cover days with no wind (important to obtain accurate data as costs and performance very sensitive to variations in windspeed).

117

- Power output (generally measured in m^4/hour: flow rate × head) proportional to the surface swept by the rotor: around $2m^4$ per m^2 swept, corresponding to $1–2m^4$ per day.

- Generally connected with a piston pump.

- Not suitable for electricity generation (see Aerogenerators p. 134).

State of maturity and commercialization

- Mechanical windpumps very old technology.

- Two main commercial types: traditional and modern lightweight multiblade (6–24 blades) to drive piston pump.

- More than 1 million installed throughout the world.

- Most windmills rated less than 10 kW. Water output function of average windspeed, rotor diameter, tower height and pumping depth.

- New designs being developed mainly in industrialized countries: lighter metal multiblade (lower capital costs and higher efficiency).

State of transferability

- Already used and produced in many countries in Asia and Latin America and some in Africa: manufactured in Argentina, Brazil, China, India, Pakistan, Senegal, etc.

- Modified cloth sail/wooden designs developed in the Netherlands, India and Colombia.

- Well proven technologies easy to transfer in the framework of national equipment programmes: transfer of know-how, setting up of production units (example: 250 persons employed at Laghouat–Algeria).

Use in rural areas

State of diffusion in developing countries

- Widespread diffusion of traditional small windmills generally with storage tanks: more than one million estimated in use world-wide.

- Cloth sail rigs traditionally used in Far East mainly for irrigation or pumping sea water for salt production.

- Large pumps can provide low-cost reliable drinking water for animals in relatively windy sites.

- New metal designs being piloted in range of developing countries (India, Pakistan, Sri Lanka, Kenya, Tunisia and Peru).

Local conditions for use

○ Adapted for 3–4m/s minimum average windspeeds.

○ Viable operation highly site specific.

○ Generally practical for pumping maximum of about 50m³/day and for 100m head.

○ Technical and social environment analysis essential before implementation.

○ Medium skills required to install (low for sail/wooden designs), to operate (mechanical drives), and to maintain (regular lubrication, replacement of sails every two years or so).

Investment and recurrent costs

○ American multiblade farm windpumps used for pumping depth 10–100m. Cost (1983) per square metre: small $150–$600 ($0.1–$0.4/m³ output), large $150–$350.

○ Manufactured in developing countries $25–$100.

Comparison with other solutions:

○ Moderate capital cost (long lifetime: around 15 years), low running costs (simple maintenance), stable wind conditions required, familiar technology.

○ Low efficiencies, high labour costs for maintenance, limited to windy sites for pump location, cannot be used for deep pumping.

Photovoltaic pumps

State of the technology

General description

○ Photovoltaic (PV) pumps are powered by electricity from a PV generator.

○ Can use DC motors (or AC motors with invertor, generally variable frequency type).

○ Can use standard equipment but special pumps/motors required to minimize system costs.

○ Generally four configurations:

— Immersed motor/centrifugal pump.

— Surface motor driving immersed pump.

— Floating motor/centrifugal pump.

— Surface mounted positive displacement pump.

○ Sizes: small (<250Wp), medium (250–2,000Wp), large (>2,000 Wp).

State of maturity and commercialization

○ Commercialized but undergoing development to reduce costs.

○ Commercialized systems: 80–5,000Wp (12–100m head, 5–500m³/day).

○ *With the sun* systems (i.e. operating only when the sun shines) with additional water storage.

○ Small-scale systems with batteries (<250Wp).

○ Standardized systems for various situations (small pumps); *kits* delivered with manual.

○ Special designs for specific conditions.

State of transferability

○ Foreign designers can work with local engineering organizations for installation and follow-up.

Use in rural areas

State of diffusion in developing countries

○ Around 1,000 pumping systems (principally medium sized) worldwide, mostly located in Francophone Africa.

○ Usually each PV pump can satisfy the water needs of 200–1,000 inhabitants.

Local conditions for use

○ Skills required to install are similar to associated pump installation (thus information required on drilling characteristics).

○ Low skills required for operation and maintenance: DC brushed motor replacement every 2,000–4,000 hours, i.e. about 2 years continuous use.

Investment and recurrent costs

○ Economics dependent on system configuration (e.g. costs and efficiencies of main components) and insolation levels.

○ High capital cost. Total installed cost between \$20 and \$30 per peak watt in 1987, for medium systems (500–1,500Wp) and \$0.3–\$0.5/m³. For example: 25 PV pumps (1400Wp each, 20m head, 35m³/day) installed in San-Mali for 25,000 people; with an installed price of \$38,000 per pump (\$27/installed Wp) the cost has been evaluated at \$0.5/m³ and \$1.8 per month per household (*GESTE*, 1988).

○ Cost of replacing DC (brushed) motor.

Comparison with other solutions

○ Generally not competitive with other technologies (e.g. diesel pumps, windmills, etc).

○ Usually not economic for water pumping for irrigation.

○ Could be competitive with diesel for very low (relatively constant) water requirements in remote areas with high insolation.

Advantages

○ High reliability (when taking into account reliability of fuel supply and spares availability for diesel pumps), low maintenance needs, low running costs.

Disadvantages

○ Minimum threshold light intensity (about 300W/m²) for pumping may not produce water output on overcast days. Water storage essential for pumps operating only *with the sun*.

ENERGY CONVERSION WITH RENEWABLE ENERGY TECHNOLOGY

Biomass densification

State of the technology

General description

○ Densification — e.g. briquetting (around 50mm diameter) or pelletizing (more difficult process, around 10mm diameter) — of high volume biomass (e.g. crop residues, agro-industrial waste products) or charcoal dust into a more useful form of fuel with greater transportabilty.

○ Reduced smoke and higher heat content per unit volume.

○ Three commercial compression methods: screw, piston and annular plate/roller granulation.

○ Hand/foot powered on household level (small scale, 5kg/h), animal — generally bullock — or motor powered (60–150kg/h) on village level (medium scale), motor powered on industrial/regional level (240–3,000kg/h).

○ Calorific value (excluding charcoal briquettes) typically around 18MJ/kg.

○ Press is only one component of the treatment process for the biomass:

— Upstream: waste preparation (drying, grinding), and in the case of charcoal, carbonization.

— Downstream: eventual carbonization, storage, transportation to industrial site (for boilers or gasifiers) or market place (for domestic use).

○ Equipment choice largely depends on waste characteristics: silica content, lignite content, granulometry, humidity content, etc.

State of maturity and commercialization

○ New designs oriented towards:

— Adaptation of designs to locally available biomass and local technical capabilities.

— Surveys of potential substitution of woodfuel through densification.

— Surveys on improvements of the total commercial chain.

State of transferability

○ Local manufacture of hand and bullock-powered presses in India, motor driven in Thailand.

○ Pilot phase in several developing countries.

○ Training for technology transfer and diffusion programmes.

State of use and diffusion in developing countries

○ Can have industrial (in boilers or gasifiers) or domestic (firewood or charcoal substitute) use.

○ Inferior to firewood and some problems (e.g. difficulty in lighting/burning, high smokiness, poor light output) can be reduced by mixing with wood.

Local conditions for use

○ Need for complete technical, economic and social survey on:

— the nature and availability of the biomass residues and potential use of densified products.

— all components of this treatment process.

○ Low skills required to install, operate and maintain for small and medium scales.

○ High skills and complete training programme required for industrial equipment.

Investment and recurrent costs

○ Range of initial cost: hand powered ($300), bullock powered ($2,500), power operated ($4,000–$13,000), industrial ($100,000).

○ Competitiveness defined by woodfuel price.

Comparison with other solutions

Densified biomass

○ Reduction in volume (higher heat content and thus decreased storage/transport costs) and in moisture content. Can use waste materials in traditional stoves.

○ Commercial production cost may be higher (binders may be required) than alternatives: not affordable by the urban poor whilst higher income groups may prefer better quality commercial fuels (kerosene, electricity, gas). May spread crop diseases. High soot level on cooking pots. Require sheltered storage (maximum humidity content 20 per cent).

Equipment

○ Small: Low capital cost but low productivity and poor quality briquettes.

○ Medium/large: High output but high capital costs.

○ Equipment has to be modified to suit situation in developing countries. High wear produced by high silica content biomass (e.g. rice husks).

Charcoal production

State of the technology

General description

○ Produced by carbonization of wood. Bark removed to reduce ash content.

○ Industrial pyrolysers: continuous operation kilns where heat is partly supplied from waste gases, and not from combustion (efficiencies up to 50 per cent).

State of maturity and commercialization

○ Mature technology in many industrialized countries.

○ Most equipment is manufactured or built locally.

○ Development of industrial methods of carbonization using various types of biomass residues.

Type of kiln	wood input (by weight)	charcoal output	conversion efficiency	time per cycle
Pit-kiln:				
Traditional	<30m³	varies	5–15%	60 days
Sheet-iron lined	<30m³	varies	<25%	—
Brick lined	<30m³	varies	<30%	—
Mound kiln:				
Traditional	30–100m³	varies	<25%	14–30 days
Casamanche(*)	1000kg	max. 280kg	<30%	—
Metal kiln:				
Mark V (TDRI)	400–400kg	—	<30%	3–5 days
Oil drum kiln	12–15kg	—	25–30%	4–8 hours
Brick kilns:				
Beehive kiln	45m³	—	25–30%	—

(*) Mound kiln modified by Swedish research mainly by improvement of flue system and addition of external chimney (Casamanche kiln); also recovers 25–30kg of wood tar per tonne of wood. New design adopted in a number of African countries.

State of transferability

○ Great amount of knowledge can still be exchanged between developing countries and industrialized countries on modern and traditional.

Use in rural areas

State of diffusion in developing countries

- ○ Widespread use of mound kilns — traditional kiln or Casamanche kiln (see above). Brick kilns common in Brazil and Argentina.

- ○ Beehive kilns used for making charcoal for iron manufacture (in Brazil); also used for brick-making and soft-coke making.

- ○ Charcoal production for urban sector where cooking fuels purchased.

Local conditions for use

- ○ High skills required to operate earth kilns (to achieve maximum conversion efficiency), all others require medium-level skills.

- ○ Low skills required to maintain Casamanche kiln.

Investment and recurrent costs

- ○ Investment costs: zero for pit/mound kiln, $200 for chimney of Casamanche kiln, $200–$5,000 for Mark V (TDRI) metal kiln, $500–$1,500 for brick kiln.

Comparison with other solutions

Product

- ○ Charcoal has higher heat content per unit mass and higher status than firewood.

- ○ Widespread acceptance as cooking/heating fuel in efficient charcoal stoves (easier to design).

- ○ Charcoal has to be kept dry. Danger of carbon monoxide poisoning if used indoors.

Conversion technology

- ○ May make a significant contribution to deforestation. Large losses in production cycle (conversion, transportation, handling).

- ○ Earth kilns have very low capital cost (spade and axe) and conversion efficiency (dependent on operator skill).

- ○ Mound kilns (and not pit kilns) can be used in areas with rock or high water table.

- ○ Lined pits can be used up to six times. Up to 30 per cent breakage loss in charcoal production; non-uniform carbonization.

- ○ Metal kilns: very high capital cost (lifetime 2 to 5 years depending on conditions) and high labour input for wood preparation (to pieces of approx 20cm × 45–60cm). High productivity (minimum cycle time 3 days), can operate during rainy weather, portable, but may accelerate deforestation.

○ Oil drum kilns: Low capital costs, but drums require frequent replacing and may be expensive/difficult to obtain. High labour input to prepare wood (maximum size 5 × 30cm), but high productivity (a skilled person can operate 10 drums twice per day).

○ Brick kilns: relatively low capital costs and long lifetime (5–8 years). Low building/maintenance skills. Produce good quality charcoal. Low wood preparation but the kiln is not transportable, requiring a large localized wood supply and long production cycle.

Biomass boilers

State of the technology

General description

○ Combustion of biomass (wood, crop residues, etc) to produce either heat (for drying purposes or hot water) or electricity (with a steam turbine) for industrial applications.

○ Fuel system can include:

— Preparation of biomass (wood or residues) when necessary: grinding, drying, densification, etc.

— Storage of feedstock.

— Transport from storage to furnace (conveyor).

— Furnace including combustion controls.

— Boiler to heat water or for steam production.

○ Under industrial conditions, efficiencies for electricity production between 15 and 20 per cent (up to 30 per cent with condensation turbines).

State of maturity and commercialization

○ Mature technology and long lifetime (estimated >15 years).

○ Available sizes: 500kW-30MW.

○ Many applications in agro-industries in developing countries.

○ Difficulties for damp and certain biomass feedstocks.

- ○ Association with local manufacturers for a gradual transfer of knowledge.

Use in rural areas

State of use and diffusion in developing countries

- ○ Widely used on an industrial scale in association with sawmills, paper production and sugar manufacture (burning bagasse).
- ○ Agro-industrial applications (drying, rice husking) with availability of low-cost biomass feedstock.
- ○ Very limited at sub-industrial scale. A few hundred (at most) in the Third World, principally in Francophone countries.
- ○ Heat production or electricity supply: electricity in excess can be fed into grid (where applicable).

Local conditions for use

- ○ Medium/high skills required to install and operate (handling and supervision staff).
- ○ Generally high skills required for regular maintenance (actual level depends on application and type of biomass utilized). Certain parts of the furnace to be replaced regularly.
- ○ Design office and engineering required for implementation: process choice determined by fuel type, availability, quantity, and compatibility with the type of needs to satisfy.

Investment and recurrent costs

- ○ Initial cost (1987) for heat production (0.5–5MW): $150,000–$600,000, and for electric power plant of 4MW electricity: $4 million. Excludes cost of the balance of equipment (fuel handling, motors, grinders, etc) which have comparable costs.
- ○ Cost of biomass depending on competition with other uses.

Comparison with other solutions

- ○ Potential substitution of indigenous biomass for imported oil.
- ○ Availability of high quality steam for process applications.
- ○ Very high capital cost. Lack of locally available skills for installation/repair.

○ Potential seasonality in availability of biomass (especially crop residues).

○ Possible diversion of biomass from other uses.

Gasifiers

State of the technology

General description

○ A gasifier with its associated gas cleaning/filtering equipment produces a low calorific value gas (comprised largely of carbon monoxide, hydrogen and nitrogen) from incomplete combustion of biomass. Gas can be burnt directly to produce heat, or used in an internal combustion engine. Three basic designs:

— Down-draught gasifiers (most common and generally used to produce stationary shaft power) produce a cleaner low calorific value (4–4.5MJ/m^3) gas. Maximum around 200kW shaft power output at present (0.5–0.6 kg of charcoal per kWh, cannot use high ash content fuels e.g. straw, rice, husks).

— Up-draught gasifiers (generally used for direct heat) produce slightly higher calorific value (5.5–6MJ/m^3) gas which contains more tars. Most suitable for direct heat applications.

— Cross-draught gasifiers (lightweight with rapid response to load thus suitable for vehicle propulsion).

○ Wood most common fuel for direct heat. Charcoal used for small-engine applications as wood tars damage engine at low outputs. Low moisture content (<20 per cent) and low ash content (<6 per cent) required for down-draught design.

○ Feedstock may require drying (a possible use of waste heat from the engine), storage (shelter), grinding, densification, and automatic feeding system.

State of maturity and commercialization

○ Widely experimented with in Europe during second World War. Pilot or experimental phase in developing countries.

○ Up to 1600kW direct heat output. Up to 200kW shaft power output. No real prospects, presently, for big (>1000kW) fluidized bed gasifiers.

○ Technology proven for charcoal and wood. Work being carried out to achieve commercial use of various maize cobs and coconut shells.

○ **Main technical** problems in extending range of biomass feedstocks to drive engine (especially using crop residues).

○ Commercial manufacture in Brazil, India, Australia, New Zealand, France, etc.

State of transferability

○ Gradual transfer to local manufacturer with boiler-making abilities (maintenance team training up to full production of equipment).

Use in rural areas

State of diffusion in developing countries

○ Largest commercial use limited to Brazil (direct heat applications include bakeries, ceramics, crop processing, foundries and chemical industries and shaft power applications in tractors and water pumping).

○ Gasifier programme in the Philippines largely halted in mid 1980s following technical and administrative difficulties.

○ Most viable application in remote forest locations for decentralized electricity supply (see p. 110) or industrial engines (e.g. sawmills, coffee plantations).

○ Commercial scale direct heat applications for industrial users (e.g. ceramics).

Local conditions for use

○ Skills to operate required for shaft power applications greater than a solid fuel boiler or conventional diesel engine (lower for direct heat applications).

○ High skills required to maintain. Frequent cleaning (one hour, once to three times a week). Maintenance training programmes required.

Investment and recurrent costs

○ Installed costs in Brazil (1982–1983):

— Down draught 30–80kW: $3,100–$3,500 (tractor engine)

— Cross-draught: $750 (diesel engine <75kW, or petrol engine <50kW)

— Up-draught 70kW: $7,500, 700kW: $30,000 (direct heat)

○ Lifetime uncertain but, with regular maintenance, estimated to be around 10,000 operational hours.

Comparison with other solutions

○ Can be used instead of petrol in engine, or substitute for 50–80 per cent for diesel in engine, or retrofit to existing diesel engines and boilers/furnaces. Lower pollution levels in emissions than conventional biomass fuel combustion methods.

○ Limited to wood or charcoal at present: economics depending on relative fuel prices. Fuels have to be pelletized. Possible negative impact on forest cover with large dissemination. Maximum power of diesel/petrol engine lowered (by around 40–50 per cent) when using gasifier. Incorrect installation (tar may condense in gas pipe between gasifier and burner) or operation will damage engine. Health and explosion hazards from fumes and waste products.

○ Operating gasifier regarded as lower status than using diesel-operated engines: increased workload for diesel operative, dirty work (due to soot in gasifier).

Biogas

State of the technology

General description

○ Anaerobic decomposition of organic matter such as manure (animal or human), crop residues and agro-industrial effluent. Production of biogas (largely methane and carbon dioxide, calorific value around $16MJ/m^3$). Digested slurry can be used as a fertilizer.

○ Digester pit volume: from 6–10m^3 (family size) up to medium (50m^3) and large units (>100m^3, up to 8MW).

○ Production: depends on type and temperature (optimum at 35°C):

— Chinese type (fixed gas dome, redesigned for continuous feed operation): 0.15–0.30m^3 of biogas per m^3 of digester and per day throughout the year (gas leakage, low efficiency).

— Indian type (floating gas dome): 0.30–0.60m^3 of biogas per m^3 of digester and per day on average;

— Plastic bag type.

○ Complex microbial processes: risk of malfunction ('shock loading') for small digesters.

State of maturity and commercialization

○ Mature technology in terms of numbers in use. Work being carried out on new designs: e.g. plug flow reactor, anaerobic baffled reactor, up-flow anaerobic sludge blanket.

○ Medium-scale commercially run biogas plant supplying energy to agro-industry (more commercially viable than community or family-sized plants).

○ Medium-scale commercially run biogas plant for electricity genera-tion using freely available feedstock: e.g. sewage or agro-industrial effluent (sugar processing or dairy plant residues).

○ Long retention time (meaning a large reactor size) for current com-mercially used technology, but advances in technology offer pros-pects for smaller reactors.

○ Methane gas only liquefies at high pressure (and cost) thus difficult to store and transport.

State of transferability

○ Exchange of knowledge and experiences mainly between developing countries. Viability conditions and acceptability varies greatly be-tween specific site conditions.

Use in rural areas

State of use and diffusion in developing countries

○ 5 million digesters in use out of 10 million installed (problems due to gas leaks and insufficient analysis of environmental conditions) in China, 1 million in India, 29,000 in Korea and less than 1,000 in other countries.

○ Generally used for cooking and lighting. Biogas can substitute for kerosene, diesel and traditional biomass cooking fuels. Biogas burns cleanly causing fewer lung and eye problems than traditional cooking fuels.

○ Digestion can eliminate pathogens in human wastes when used as the feedstock, but there are often taboos against this.

○ Nitrogenous fertilizer by-product.

Local conditions for use

○ Reduced gas output in winter.

○ Technology viable for high income groups.

○ Feedstocks depend on local availability and social acceptability. Labour intensive for provision of dung and water feedstock. High

131

feedstock cost may lead to low eocnomic returns (if manure is already sold as in parts of India for fertilizer and cooking fuel).

Skills required	Chinese type	Indian type
to install	High: dome building to obtain gas tight gas seal	Easier construction but metal gas holder is workshop built
to operate	Low: labour intensive to load and clean pit(1)	Low: little operational labour
to maintain	Low: wall relining when leaks appear	Low: drum painting 2–3 years

(1) The new *batch* design has lower labour requirements

Investment and recurrent costs

○ Chinese type, 8m³ family unit: $100–$200 (1984).

○ Indian type, 8–10m³ family unit with steel drum: $250–$800 (1984).

Hydro plants

State of the technology

General description

○ Conversion of potential energy in water (at elevated height: 1.5 up to 400m) to shaft and/or electrical power with overall theoretical efficiency 60–80 per cent (can retrofit turbines to existing mechanical output units).

○ Main components: water penstock, control system, turbine (plus generator if electrical output).

○ Size depend on local climate, geographical factors and power demand: micro (<100kW), mini (100–500kW), small (500–1,000kW), large (>1,000kW).

○ Three principal turbine types depending on flow and water height: reaction (Francis, Kaplan), or impulse (traditional water wheel, Pelton).

○ Complete installation requires: water supply infrastructure, the turbine, generator, and, for electricity production, distribution lines and a regulation system (adaptation of production to electricity demand).

State of maturity

○ Mature, much experience available in industrialized and developing countries.

○ On-going improvements concern electronic regulating devices, sizing methods and manufacture techniques.

State of transferability

○ Local manufacture in number of developing countries principally in Asia and Latin America.

○ Transfer of know-how through association with local designers (follow-up and maintenance) and, if sufficient market, with local manufacturers.

Use in rural areas

State of diffusion in developing countries

○ Widespread diffusion, especially Asia and Latin America. China (in 1983) had 76,000 small hydro plants with a total installed capacity 8,500MW.

○ Most viable application for micro/mini hydro: areas where grid extension or large hydro have too high a cost. Mechanical shaft power and electricity production: day-time (on-site) use of mechanical power by small-scale agro-industries (grinding, sawing, oil pressing, rice hulling), or water lifting (see p. 113) and electricity supply for evening uses.

Local conditions for use

○ Knowledge of local hydrological resources (simple methods can be used if no data available) and physical constraints (usually 5km maximum for plant to electricity utilization).

○ Low/medium skills required for civil works, higher for turbine (and generator) installation and increases rapidly with size.

○ Low skills required to operate. Medium to maintain (increases with size). Considered very reliable, but requiring regular routine inspection.

Investment and recurrent costs

○ Costs depend on location and application. Equipment costs for small hydro usually about 30 per cent of total.

○ Locally manufactured (10kW) micro-hydro in Nepal (1981): equipment cost $2,600, total cost $6,000. Locally manufactured micro-

133

hydro in Argentina (1986) cost per kW installed $3,576 (with line), $2,573 (without line). Imported equipment for 20–500kW: $8,000–$2,000 per kW installed.

Comparison with other solutions

Costs

○ No fuel requirements and low maintenance. Potentially high local content for capital costs.

○ High capital costs (equipment and electricity transmission and distribution). Often high operating costs (due to over-staffing, improper maintenance and breakdowns) and low load factors (thus high generation costs) common for small units.

3Equipment and environment

○ Simple design/installation. For micro/small hydro projects a short lead time from design to commissioning. Power output can be up-rated through incremental technical change. Generally simple operation (lower than comparable sized thermal plant). Also water infrastructure can give food control. No environmental problems in short term.

○ Viability highly site specific. Requires constant water flow (unless there are storage facilities). May conflict with irrigation water needs.

Photovoltaic generators

State of the technology

General description

○ Photovoltaic (PV) devices convert solar radiation into direct current (DC) electricity. PV cells are manufactured from silicon and produce very small voltage (0.6V). A PV module interconnects a group of 15 to 30 cells. A PV panel comprises one or two modules. An array comprises several panels.

○ Arrays are set up at a specific angle to sun (fixed arrays) or continually adjusted to remain perpendiular to sun (tracking arrays of concentrating devices with mirrors or lenses).

○ A complete system includes:

— The PV generator itself, which can be connected directly to equipment that operates only *with the sun*,

- Regulator and batteries, when electricity storage is necessary (lighting, radio, refrigerators, etc),

- Invertor to convert DC current into AC current when required by equipment;

- (Generally) special equipment adapted to match what is in effect a *very expensive* source of energy. Examples include special electric pumps, highly insulated refrigerators, high efficiency appliances (lighting), etc.

○ Power output is given in peak watt (Wp): output at 25°C under a light intensity of 1kW/m². A typical module (0.3m × 0.5m) containing 36 cells would produce 30–35W DC current at 12 volts in bright sunshine (supply about 10Wh/day in Dakar-Senegal in January, sufficient for three lights for three hours).

○ Size: small (10–200Wp), medium (200–5,000Wp) and large (>500Wp).

State of maturity and commercialization

○ Fully commercialized even if costs have not fallen as rapidly as anticipated. Potentially long lifetime (about 20 years) and generally 5–10 year warranty.

○ Generally silicon cells although there is a shift to amorphous form. Polycrystalline or amorphous devices, less costly per unit of surface than single crystal, have a lower efficiency, and thus the same cost per peak watt.

○ Currently widely used for very small power needs (e.g. watches, calculators, consumer goods) and in remote power systems.

○ Small generators (10–160Wp): easy-to-assemble kits with manual. Medium scale (200–5,000Wp): qualified installer required.

○ See p. 147 for special batteries and appliances.

State of transferability

○ Very high technology, cannot be manufactured locally, except for some parts of the system (among developing countries only India and Brazil produce solar cells).

Use in rural areas

State of diffusion in developing countries

○ Most viable for small loads in remote sites with high insolation levels without grid connection, where supplies of diesel/petrol unreliable, or with electricity consumption levels not exceeding a few kWh/day.

- Ideally suited to unmanned operation due to high reliability.

- Three types of suitable applications: rural pre-electrification (see p. 110), solar pumps (see p. 119) or specialized use (communications, pipeline protection, beacons, etc).

Local conditions for use

- Medium to very high skills required to install depending on the size.

- Low but reliable skills required to operate and to maintain: battery maintenance (replacement every 3 to 7 years), routine inspection, regular cleaning of plate collector, and replacement of defective parts. Remote systems inspection typically six months.

- Require some changes in user's habits (efficient use of electricity through information and training) and the purchase of high-efficiency appliances. Regional programmes for collective appliances and maintenance teams.

Investment and recurrent costs

- Module price from the producer is still very high: $2 to $5 per peak watt depending on the quantity delivered. Costs projected to fall over next decade through economies of scale and improved production techniques.

- The cost of the total system (excluding end-use equipment) could be more than twice the cost of the panels (domestic use, 30–500Wp: $20–$30/Wp). Lighting kits with fluorescent lamps: $500–$1,500. Solar battery chargers: $45-$250.

- Low running costs (no fuel supply).

Advantages

- Competitive with diesel-generated electricity in remote areas where there is a demand for small amounts of power (e.g. battery charging, medical refrigerators, remote telecommunications repeater station).

- Clean energy source, modular technology, low running costs and low maintenance, potentially long life.

Disadvantages

- Very high capital costs (foreign exchange), no economies of scale, provision of electricity only during day-time (need of batteries with 3 to 7 year lifetime, except for systems that operate only with the sun), expensive and complex invertors when AC current is needed for standard appliances.

Solar water heaters

State of the technology

General description

○ Utilization of solar energy for heating water usually to 40–60°C (directly or via heat exchanger).

○ Up to three main components: flat plate collector, heat transfer circuit and (ideally insulated) storage reservoir.

○ Collector usually comprises absorber (blackened metal plate with metal tubing) in an insulated box with glass cover. Water circulation by either natural or (via pump) forced convection. Water heated by collector raises temperature of water in storage tank (via heat exchanger) or feeds directly into tank.

○ Auxiliary heating could be required for secure adequate supply.

○ Output depending on collector area (modular) and insolation level. Daily output typically 100 litres of *warm* water per square metre of collector area on an *average* sunny day.

State of maturity and commercialization

○ Mature technology but large-scale units can be difficult to interface with plumbing systems (standards set up in some industrialized countries, e.g. in France: NF P50/501).

○ Commercial use principally limited to industrialized countries at present.

○ Potentially long lifetime (10 to 25 years), often 10 year warranty.

State of transferability

○ Can be produced locally by local manufacturers through:

— Training for assembly, maintenance and servicing.

— Creation of production units (capital costs for a production of 5,000m² of collector per year: around $150,000, according to *GESTE*, 1988).

— Already accomplished transfer in Egypt, Maghreb, Niger, Senegal, the Seychelles, etc. In 1985, Zimbabwe was exporting complete systems to USA.

Use in rural areas

State of use and diffusion in developing countries

○ Mainly in urban areas where electricity is expensive.

○ Hot water supplies to hospitals and hotels (sanitary uses: showers, washing, cleaning, etc), or industries (e.g. food processing).

Local conditions for use

○ Low skills required to operate and maintain (cleaning collector surface, water quality, joints, etc) if well constructed.

○ General plumbing skills required increase with scale and complexity.

○ If no back-up system available, require some changes in user's habits if optimization of solar energy collected is expected.

Investment and recurrent costs

○ 1987 prices from the producer: $700–$1,000 (80-litre capacity) and £1,500–$1,800 (100-litre capacity).

○ Lower capital costs when produced locally.

Comparison with other solutions

○ Can be produced locally, and reduce (commercial) fuel expenditures.

○ High capital cost, fragility of glass, depends on solar insolation.

Solar driers

State of the technology

General description

○ Solar driers classified according to three features: direct or indirect sun; mode of air flow (commonly used natural convection, or forced convection with fan), and separate or combined solar collector/drier.

— Direct solar driers: the crop exposed to sun, drying rates higher as heat transfer by both convection and radiation.

— Indirect solar driers: the crop is placed in a drying chamber, heat transfer by convection only, used where direct exposure would reduce vitamin C content of certain produce or to avoid bleaching action of the sun.

○ Three most common designs (can be built to required size, generally 1m^2 per 10kg of fresh produce):

— Type I: direct drying with natural convection and combined collector/drying chamber (cabinet drier, tent drier). Tent drier: 3 days for drying fish (5 days for traditional drying).

— Type II: as type I but with separate collector/drier chamber (chimney drier).

— Type III: indirect heating, forced convection and separate collector/drying chamber (industrial scale operation).

○ Very little data in the literature for the technology or the acceptability of dried produce (especially cash crops).

○ Expected efficiencies vary by factors of up to ten.

State of maturity and commercialization

○ Principles well understood. Apart from some commercial uses in developing countries, technology largely at demonstration phase.

State of transferability

○ Exchanges of experiences between developing countries, but each technology has to be re-considered according to local conditions, traditions and actual market conditions.

Use of rural areas

State of diffusion in developing countries

○ Generally most viable for medium (co-operative) and large-scale operation (industrial level) for high value produce (chillies, raisins, tobacco, fish).

○ Large scale use of solar driers for fruit (figs, raisins and dates) in Argentina, Brazil, Portugal and Turkey. Natural convection driers considered to be widespread (most commonly cabinet drier followed by tent drier).

○ Cabinet drier used for drying vegetables and some types of fruit (grapes). Extensive experimental/pilot test work on cabinet drier in Jamaica.

○ Tent drier developed in Bangladesh for drying fish. Modified and used in tropics and India.

○ Experimental work on Type II carried out by Asian Institute of Technology (Thailand). Extension work (under ILO auspices) to promote solar driers carried out in Sudan.

139

Local conditions for use

○ Low skills required to operate. Low skills to install and maintain for type I, much higher for Types II and III.

Investment and recurrent costs

○ Chimney drier: $100 plus 6 person days labour (excluding bamboo poles).

Comparison with other solutions

Advantages

○ Designs relatively simple, faster drying rates, and very low running costs (much less attention required than sun drying). Produces improved and more consistent quality product:

— Lower final moisture content,

— Reduced risk of spoilage (during drying and subsequent storage),

— Reduced risk of infestation by insects or microbes,

— Protection from insects, dust and animals (provided by drying structure).

Disadvantages

○ May have high capital cost (uncertain lifetime in field conditions). Users may purchase alternative (lower cost) drying methods (diesel or electric drier): artificial drying generally used when ambient drying not possible (in multiple cropping, cold/wet weather in post harvest season), existing driers require manual handling of product and generally inappropriate for large throughput (except for large commercial driers).

○ Chimney drier: stability problems in windy conditions, high cost plastic sheet, difficult to dismantle and store after use without damaging plastic.

Aerogenerators

State of the technology

General description

○ Conversion of wind energy to (AC or DC) electricity.

○ High speed rotor with 2 or 3 blades (slow speed windmills not suitable: e.g. multiblades, Savonius, etc) and safety mechanism to avoid damage in high wind conditions.

○ Electricity storage as buffer against variability in wind.

○ No electricity storage required when connected to equipment that only operates *with the wind* (e.g. with an electric pump, water storage may be required).

○ Complex machines requiring suitable skilled environment, consisting of:

— The rotor and the safety mechanism,

— The generator to convert shaft power into AC or DC current,

— A tower allowing maintenance and repairs,

— A control device to adapt power to utilization needs, or connection to the grid or back-up system.

State of maturity and commercialization

Classification	Diameter	Power
small	<7m	<10kW
medium	7–8m	10–20kW
large	8–12m	20–50kW
very large	>12m	<50kW

Variation in the definition of size in the literature.

○ No manufacturers in developing countries (apart from China and India).

○ Mature for small size.

○ Experimental/pilot phase in industrialized countries (research being carried out to design aerogenerators with outputs >1MW and high speed vertical axis generators).

○ Research for adaptation to low windy sites of Savonius and Darrieus rotors (vertical axis).

State of transferability

○ Complex and sophisticated technology.

○ Technical expertise required to select/size/adapt the technology.

141

Use in rural areas

State of use and diffusion in developing countries

○ Small: Demonstration projects in some developing countries.

○ Medium: Being piloted in developing countries to provide power for telecommunication equipment (radio telephone repeaters), marine light beacons, or feed into grid at remote site (wind farms), on remote sites with regular and high wind regime. Commercial scale for recharging batteries (e.g. boats).

○ Large: Limited to a few industrialized countries to feed into grid (more than 1,000 MW in USA, more than 400 MW in Denmark).

Local conditions for use

○ Wind regime (and thus economic viability) highly site-dependent: sheltered areas (e.g. valleys, close to forests, buildings) generally unsuitable whilst hilltop more ideal.

○ Use requires precise evaluation of wind potential, including variability.

○ From medium to extremely high skills are required for installation and maintenance (qualified technicians to replace wearing parts) according to the design and the size: ten years of estimated lifetime and (bi)annual inspections.

Investment and recurrent costs

○ Investment costs: $1,000–$20,000 per kW installed at 10m/s (foreign exchange). For example: aerogenerator plant at Tromelin, La Reunion, 2 × 10kW aerogenerators with batteries and invertor, produce around 20,000Wh/year, initial costs $170,000.

Comparison with other solutions

○ Economic at windy sites. Minimum monthly average windspeed required: >4 to 5m/s (excludes large areas of the world).

○ Less prone to theft than other devices (e.g. diesel engines).

○ Speedy access to high technical skills required (difficult to diagnose equipment failures).

○ High capital cost.

○ High variability of windspeed requires batteries (or large number of aerogenerators).

ENERGY CONSERVATION

Improved woodfuel stoves

General description

- ○ Aimed to replace traditional stoves/fireplaces used by rural poor or urban people. Generally made from mud (usually by user) or ceramic (i.e. fireclay) by trained artisan.

- ○ Ceramic (i.e. pottery liner) stoves can be covered with mud to decrease heat losses, but this reduces the efficiency for short duration cooking (increased heat capacity).

- ○ Mud stoves generally very heavy and not portable. Chimney can be added (increased cost) to decrease smoke in kitchen. Two basic design types: one-pot and multipot (typically two or three pot holders).

- ○ Lifetime: 1 to 2 years for ceramic designs, slightly longer for mud stoves.

State of use and diffusion in developing countries

- ○ Objectives: save fuel, save time (higher cooking speed), reduce smoke, have modern image, increase employment for potters (stove and spares). Improve nutrition (faster cooking, less vitamin loss according to some nutritionists). Very few examples of fuel savings in field use reported in literature. Significant impact on deforestation being questioned.

- ○ Large-scale diffusion programmes in China, India and Sri Lanka.

- ○ Stove programmes generally failed to achieve widespread diffusion in rural areas for technical, social and economic reasons. Failure to take into account site specificity and user needs (e.g. space heat, light, smoke) by developing stoves in isolation from end user. Importance of project design (e.g. carrying out feasibility studies, monitoring and evaluation, piloting designs) beginning to be recognized.

- ○ For rural poor, new stoves involve monetary costs to obtain non-financial benefits, may not be more efficient than traditional designs, and may not fit in with traditional cooking practices. Smoke may not be a problem (e.g. curing food, deterring insects).

Local conditions for use

- ○ Mud stoves difficult to construct (even by trained builders); fewer difficulties for ceramic design. Lifetime may be short.

143

○ Operation is simple for one-pot stoves, skills are required for several dampers and pot holes. Frequent repair to cracking in mud stoves.

Most viable applications

○ Urban sector where cooking fuels are bought.

○ Heavy fuel-users: food sellers, institutions (schools, health centres, etc).

Investment and recurrent costs

○ Estimated construction time of half to one day for mud stoves plus purchase of chimney (usually largest cost component).

○ Ceramic stove: around US$2 (1987) in Sri Lanka per pot holder.

Improved charcoal stoves

General description

○ Improved designs (higher efficiency than traditional charcoal stoves) generally for use in urban sector promoted from early 1980s. Referred to as improved jiko – Swahili word for traditional charcoal stove.

○ Comprise ceramic (cement or vermiculite) insert with metal lining (based on traditional charcoal stove used in Thailand – Thai Bucket).

○ Output depends on charcoal burning rate.

State of diffusion in developing countries

○ Improved design largely disseminated in Kenya. Already in widespread use in Thailand. More than 100,000 disseminated by mid-1980s.

○ Most viable in urban sector where charcoal is purchased and used as cooking fuel.

Local conditions for implementation

○ Low skills to install, operate and maintain (but low lifetime of grates).

Advantages

○ Low capital cost (fast payback time). Fuel saving.

○ Portable. Faster cooking.

Disadvantages

○ Size only suitable for domestic cooking.

○ Clay grates crack frequently (around 2 to 3 months).

○ Difficult to light charcoal when using clay grates.

Internal combustion engines

General description

○ Diesel engines: can provide shaft or electric power (single or three phase).

○ Diesel generator sets: shaft power by compression engines from 0.5kW up to several tens of megawatts.

○ Explosion or controlled ignition engines (kerosene or gasoline fed): from 0.5 up to 5kW.

○ Fuel consumption: typical figures are 0.3–0.6 litre of gasoline per kWh (or equivalent: 0.2–0.4 litre per hour and per horse power).

○ When used at a fraction of the nominal capacity, fuel consumption can increase 20 per cent at half speed, 60 per cent at quarter speed.

State of maturity and commercialization

○ Fully commercialized.

○ Research and development for adaptation to other fuels (gas from gasifiers, biogas, alcohol, vegetable oils or esters, etc). Engines already available for some of the fuels.

State of transferability

○ Local manufacture in many developing countries.

Use in rural areas

State of diffusion in developing countries

○ In 1985, estimated 3.5 million diesel engines in India for irrigation pumping alone.

○ Very widely disseminated, wide range of tasks:

— Very small (<5hp): Portable power sources (pumpsets, electricity generation).

— Small (5–30hp): Agriculture machinery (small tractors and power tillers), stationary electric power generating sets, fishing boats, road rollers.

- Medium (30–100hp): Electric generating sets, dumpers, medium/large tractors, marine engines (fishing boats).

- Large (100–500hp): Earth-moving equipment, main propulsion units marine cargo ships or off-shore fishing.

- Very large (>400hp): Railway engines, generating sets, marine propulsion units.

Local conditions for use

○ Medium skills required to install, operate and maintain.

○ Need for constant servicing and supervision by a trained person: checking, filling of fuel tank, starting and stopping processes, periodic adjustments and repairs (every 500 hours or less).

○ Electric generators sets suitable if:

- Good technical environment,

- Availability of fuel, lubricants and spare parts, and reliability in distribution,

- High and regular demand.

Investment and recurrent costs

○ For village electrification, irregular demand generally requires two units for maintenance.

○ Ex-factory prices 1–5kW (gasoline): $500–$250/kW. 1–500kW (diesel): $700–$100/kW.

○ Some required options such as trailer, etc, can double these prices,

○ Other costs: transportation, civil engineering, installation, storage, and connection to the local grid.

Comparison with other solutions

○ Widespread technology. Relatively low capital cost. Portable and simple to use.

○ Lifetime 10,000–40,000 hours for 50–500kW.

○ High operating cost: oversizing and low loading rate can be responsible for 20–80 per cent of kWh cost.

○ Require reliable fuel and lubricating oil supplies.

Appliances for photovoltaic generators

Batteries

○ Sealed lead storage batteries: Good efficiency (low self-discharge rate) and no maintenance required. Suitable for low storage (100–300Ah) and limited number of cycles (charge/discharge).

○ Pure lead stationary batteries: Modular, 2 volt-elements connected in series. Low discharge rate. Maintenance: addition of electrolyte once or twice a year. Suitable for great number of cycles (charge/discharge) and storage up to several thousands Ah.

○ Cadmium/Nickel batteries: More expensive but lighter and long lifetime. Suitable for low power levels (portable lights, radio-sets, etc.).

○ Charge regulators: Special regulators adapted to photovoltaic generation of electricity. Prices in France: 5–100A regulators for 12 or 24V DC current, $100–1,000.

Lighting appliances

○ Low consumption: high efficiency fluorescent lamps consuming 3–4 times less current than incandescent bulbs. Some indications of prices in France (1987):

    ○ Portable rechargeable lights with Cadmium/Nickel battery, $100.

    ○ Fluorescent mini-strips 6–13W: $50–$70.

    ○ Fluorescent light fittings 8–40W: around $55 (powered through a special device: around $50).

Pumps for photovoltaic generator

○ With the sun pumps (i.e. with no need for batteries):

    — Surface pumps, 60–500m^3/day, 5–15m lift, $7,000–$13,000.

    — Immersed moto-pump, 10–200m^3/day, 10-110m depth, $14,000–$55,000.

○ Submersible impulsor pumps, 0.3m^3/hour, 25m depth, $350.

Solar refrigerators and deep-freezers

○ More expensive than common equipment but better insulated (refrigerator: 300–500Wh/day for 200 litres, deep-freezer: 750Wh/day for 300 litres). Indicative prices: 40–300 litre: $1,000–$1,500.

Invertors

○ Conversion of DC current (12, 24 or 48V) from the photovoltaic generator into AC current (50 Hz, 220V) for use of available standard and cheaper appliances. Invertors are expensive ($150–$400 for 60–300Wp) and require larger surfaces of solar panels (variable efficiencies up to less than 50 per cent, implying double the number of panels).

Annex III: Bibliography

Abbie, L., Harrison, J.Q. and J.W. Wall, (1982), *Economic Returns to Investment in Irrigation*, World Bank Staff Working Paper 536, World Bank, Washington, D.C.

Adams, D.C. and D.H. Graham, (1981), 'A critique of traditional agricultural credit projects and policies', *Journal of Development Economics*, 8(3), pp. 347–366.

Adams, D.C. and R.C. Vogel, (1986), 'Rural financial markets in low income countries: recent controversies and lessons', *World Development*, 14(4), pp. 477–487.

Adams, D.C. *et al.* (ed.), (1984), *Undermining Rural Development with Cheap Credit*, Westview Press, Boulder, Colorado.

AFME (1984), *Energie et transports: monographies par pays: Maroc, Corée du Sud, Brésil, Mexique, Indonésie, Equateur*, Transenerg, BCEOM, Paris, France.

AFME (1985), *Gazogènes et plantations intensives de bois dans les programmes d'irrigation*, AFME, Paris, France.

AFME (1985), *Vivez eau solaire*, AFME, Paris, France.

AFME (1986), *L'électricité photovoltaïque: applications multiples*, AFME, Paris, France.

AFME (1986) *La mise en oeuvre des programmes de pompage photovoltaïque*, AFME, Paris, France.

AFME (1986), *Les petites centrales hydro-électriques*, AFME, Paris, France.

AFME (1987), *Cultures énergétiques et gazogènes*, AFME, Paris, France.

AFME (1987), *L'électricité solaire: la solution photovoltaïque*, Paris, France.

AFME (1987), *La diffusion des chauffe-eau solaires thermosiphons dans les DOM-TOM*, AFME, Paris, France.

AFME Kompass, (no date), *Catalogue des matériels, systèmes, ingéniérie et services français en maîtrise de l'énergie* Ed° SNEI-KOMPASS, Paris, France.

AFME, Asencio S., (no date), *Electrification rurale photovoltaïque dans les DOM-TOM* AFME-GRET-GERES-Ministère de la Coopération, Paris, France.

AFME, Bellami J.J., C. Ducos, M. Joly, P.B. Joly (1984), *Guide technique de la densification*, AFME-ABF, Paris, France.

AFME, Briane D. & Doat J. (1985), *Guide technique de la carbonisation: la fabrication du charbon de bois* AFME, EDISUD, Aix-en-Provence, France.

149

AFME, Cornut, B., de Gromard C. (1986), *La pré-électrification rurale solaire*, AFME, Paris, France.

AFME, Courty P. (1985), *Abrégé de carbonisation* AFME-GRET-Ministère de la Coopération, Paris, France.

AFME, de Gromard C. & B. Cornut (1987), 'La pré-électrification rurale solaire', *7° conférence sur le photovoltaïque de Séville*, AFME, Paris, France.

AFME, Louvel R. (1985), *Projet pilote domestique de briquettes au Niger* AFME-ABF, Paris, France.

AFME, Louvel R. (1986), *La densification des résidus végétaux dans les pays en développement* ABF, Rapport pour l'AFME, Paris, France.

AFME-CAS (1986 & 1987), *Colloques* 'Des watts pour la vie: marchés et produits photovoltaïques d'aujourd'hui', AFME, Paris, France.

AFME-CETIAT (1984), *Les chaudières à bois de moins de 500kW*, AFME, Paris, France.

AFME-CSTB (1984), *Les chauffe-eau solaires individuels en climat*, Ed° du CSTB, Paris, France.

AFME-GRET, Billerey (1984), *La pompage photovoltaïque*, GRET-GERES-AFME, Paris, France.

AFME-Ministère de la Coopération (no date), *Systèmes photovoltaïques pour les pays en développement: manuel d'installation et d'utilisation* La Documentation Française, Paris, France.

AFME-SEMA-MRE/CODEV (1982), *Energies renouvelables au Sahel: Evaluation des projets* La Documentation Française, Paris, France.

Agarwal, B. (1983), 'Diffusion of rural innovations: some analytical issues and the case of wood-burning stoves, *World Development*, 11(4A), pp. 359–376.

Agarwal, B. (1986), *Cold Hearths and Barren Slopes: The Woodfuel Crisis in the Third World*, Institute of Economic Growth, Delhi.

Ahmad, I. (1985), *Technology and Rural Women in the Third World, World Employment Programme*, International Labour Office, Geneva, Switzerland.

Akrich, M. (1988a), 'Etude de Cas: Le compacteur à briquettes de coton de Chinandega au Nicaragua' in *Détermination des facteurs socio-culturels dans la planification énergétique des pays en développement*, Commission of the European Communities (CEC)-DGE, 86-B-7060-11-007-17, Brussels.

Akrich, M. (1988b), 'Etude de cas: Le gazogène de Buena vista au Costa Rica', in *Détermination des facteurs socio-culturels dans la planification énergétique des pays en développement*, CEC-DGE, 86-B-7060-11-007-17, Brussels.

Alam, M. and J. Dunkery, (1983), *Fuelwood survey in Hyderabad*, Resources for the Future, Washington, D.C.

Anderson, C. (1986), 'Declining tree stocks in African countries', *World Development*, 14(7), pp. 853–63.

Anderson, D. and R. Fishwick, (1984), 'Fuelwood consumption and deforestation in African countries', *World Bank Staff Working Paper Number 704*, Washington, D.C.

Anderson, D. (1987), *The Economics of Afforestation: A Case Study in Africa*, Occasional Paper Number 1, The World Bank, Johns Hopkins University Press, Baltimore.

Ashworth, J. (1985), *Renewable Energy Systems in Asia: Current Success and the Potential for Future Widespread Dissemination*, Bureau for Asia, U.S. Agency for International Development, Washington, D.C.

Asia and Pacific Development Centre, (1985), *Integrated Energy Planning: A Manual*, (4 volumes), Kuala Lumpur, Malaysia.

Asia and Pacific Development Centre, (1988), *Rural Energy Planning*, Kuala Lumpur, Malaysia.

Ayres, R.C. (1983), *Banking on the poor: the World Bank and Rural Poverty*, MIT Press, Cambridge, Massachusetts.

Baily, M.A. (1980), 'Brickmaking in Colombia: a case study of alternative technologies', *World Development*, 1980.

Bangladesh Institute of Development Studies – Dhaka International Food Policy Research Institute (1986), *Credit for alleviation of rural poverty – The experience of the Grameen Bank in Bangladesh*, Dhaka.

Barker, R. *et al.* (1973), 'Employment and technical change in Philippine agriculture', in *Mechanisation and employment in agriculture*, ILO, Geneva.

Barnard, G. & C. Zaror, (1986), 'Industries du Tiers-Monde consommatrices de bois de feu', in *Le Courrier*, No. 95, CEC, Brussels.

Barnett, A., Pyle, L. and S.K. Subrarian, (1978), *Biogas Technology in the Third World: A multidisciplinary review*, International Development Research Centre, Ottawa.

Barnett, A. (ed.), (1990), *The Diffusion of Rural Energy Technologies*, World Development, Special Issue, Vol 18 No 4, April, Pergamon Press.

Barwell, I., Edmonds, G.A. Howe, J.D.G.F. and J. de Veen (1985), *Rural; Transport in Developing Countries*, International Labour Organisation, Geneva.

Bates, R.H. (1981), *Markets and States in Tropical Africa: the Political Bias of Agricultural Policies*, University of California Press, Berkeley.

Beenhakker, H.L., Carapetis, S., Crowther, L. and S. Hertel (1987), *Rural Transportation Services: A Guide to their Planning and Implementation*, Intermediate Technology Publications Ltd, London.

Bernardo, Francisco P. and Gregorio U Kilayko, (1990), 'Promoting Rural Energy Technology: The Case of Gasifiers in the Philippines', *World Development*, Vol 18 No 4, 10 pages, Pergamon Press.

Bhatia, R. (1984a),'Energy and agriculture in developing countries', *Energy Research Group Paper Number 56*, International Development Research Centre, Ottawa, September.

Bhatia, R. (1984b), *Energy Alternatives for Irrigation Pumping: An Economic Analysis for Northern India*, World Employment Programme Working Paper (WEP 2-22/WP 137), International Labour Office, Geneva.

151

Bhatia, R. (1985), 'Photovoltaic lighting in Fiji', in *Applications of New Technologies to Small-Scale Activities*, World Employment Programme, International Labour Office, Geneva.

Bhatia, R. (1987), *Economic Evaluation and Diffusion of Renewable Energy Technologies: Case Studies from India*, Manuscript report, IDRC-MR162e, International Development Research Centre, Ottawa, October.

Bhatia, R. and A.F. Pereira (eds), (1988), *Socioeconomic Aspects of Renewable Energy Technologies*, Praeger, New York.

Bhatia, R. (1987), *Institutional Aspects of Promoting Renewable Energy Technologies in India*, WEP 2-22/WP 177, International Labour Office, Geneva.

Bialy, J. (1986), *A new approach to domestic fuelwood conservation: Guidelines for research*, Women in Agricultural Production and Rural Development Service, Human Resources, Institutions and Agrarian Reform Division, Food and Agriculture Organisation, Rome.

Biggs, S. and C.E. Burns (1977), 'The changing rural economy of northeastern India', Institute of Development Studies, University of Sussex, Brighton, UK.

Biggs, S.D. and E.J. Burns, (1983), *Generation and Diffusion of Agricultural Technology: A Review of Theories and Experiences*, WEP 2-22/WP 122, International Labour Office, Geneva.

Binswanger, H.P. (1987), *The Economics of Tractors in South Asia: An Analytical Review*, Agricultural Development Council, New York.

Binswanger, H.P. (1984), 'Agricultural mechanisation: a comparative historical perspective', *World Bank Staff Working Paper Number 673*, World Bank, Washington, D.C.

Biomasse Actualité (1985), *Numéro spécial No. 7* 'La combustion', Paris, France.

Biomasse Actualité (1986), *Numéro spécial* 'Le Biogaz', Paris, France.

Biomasse Actualité (1986), *Numéro spécial* 'Les gazogènes', Paris, France.

Birgergard, L. (1988), 'A review of experiences with Integrated Rural Development', *Manchester Papers on Development*, IV(1), p 4–27, January.

Bonfils, M. (1987), *Halte à la désertification au Sahel*, Ed° Karthala, Paris, France.

Braverman, A. and J.L. Gausch, (1986), 'Rural credit markets and institutions in developing countries: lessons for policy analysis from practice and modern theory', *World Development*, 14(10/11), pp. 1253–1267.

Briscoe, J. (1979), 'Energy use and social structures in a Bangladesh village', *Population and Development Review*, 5(4), December.

Brown, T.G. (1977), 'Politique des prix agricoles et croissance économique', in *Finance et Développement*.

Bruggink, J.J.C. (1984), *The Socio-economic Aspects of Introducing Solar Flat Plate Collector Technology in the Sahel*, World Employment Programme Working Paper (WEP 2-22/WP130), International Labour Office, Geneva.

Butin, V. (1987), *Bois irrigués et Gazogènes, Etudes de cas en Inde*, AFME-GRET-Ministère de la Coopération, Paris, France.

152

Carapetis, S., Beenhakker, H.L. and J.D.F. Howe, (1984), 'The supply and quality of rural transportation services in developing countries: a comparative review', *World Bank Staff Working Paper Number 654*, World Bank, Washington, D.C.

CDI, (1980), *Microcentrales utilisant les énergies renouvelables pour les pays ACP*, CDI, Brussels.

Cecelski, E. (1985), *The rural energy crisis, women's work and basic needs: Perspectives and approaches to action*, Technical Cooperation Report, Rural Employment Policy Research Programme, International Labour Office, Geneva, 1985.

Cecelski, E. (1987), 'Energy and rural women's work: Crisis, response and policy alternatives', *International Labour Review*, 126(1), pp. 41–64, January–February 1987.

CEEMAT (1975), *Manuel de culture avec traction animale*, Ed° Ministére de la Coopération, Paris, France.

CEEMAT (1982), 'Energies renouvelables. Applications à l'agriculture des pays chauds', *Machinisme Agricol Tropical* No. 80, Antony, France.

CEMAGREF (1979), 'Evaluation des quantités d'eau nécessaires aux irrigations', La Documentation Française, Paris, France.

Cernea, M. (1985), 'Alternative units of social organisation sustaining afforestation strategies', in M. Cernea (ed.), *Putting people first: Sociological variables in rural development*, Oxford University Press, Oxford.

Cernea, Michael (ed.) (1985), *Putting People First: Sociological Variables in Rural Development*, Oxford University Press, Oxford.

Chambers, R. (1980), 'Le petit paysan est un professionel', in *CERES* mars/avril 1980, Paris, France.

Chambers, R. and M. Leach, (1987), 'Trees to meet contingencies: Savings and security for the rural poor', Network Paper 5a, Social Forestry Network, Overseas Development Institute, London, October.

Chambers, R. (1983), *Rural Development: Putting the Last First*, Longman, London.

Chambers, R. (1989), *Développement rural* Ed° Karthala, Paris, France.

CIDA and others, (1987), *Handbook for the Comparative Evaluation of Technical and Economic Performance by Water Pumping Systems*, CIDA/DGIS/USAID/FAO.

CIEH, (no date), 'Le point d'eau au village', La Documentation Française, Paris, France.

CIEH-Diluca, (no date), *Pompes à main en hydraulique villageoise*, La Documentation Française, Paris, France.

CIFOPE, (1986), *Séminaire sur la politique énergétique en Afrique, Lomé*, Publication ACCT-CIFOPE, Paris, France.

Clay, E.J. (1982), 'Technical innovation and public policy: agricultural development in the Kosi Region, Bihar, India', *Agricultural Administration*, 9, pp. 189–210.

Clément, J. & S. Strafogel, (no date), *Disparition de la forêt, quelles solutions à la crise du bois de feu en Afrique?* L'Harmattan, Paris, France.

Cohen, J.M. (1980), 'Integrated Rural Development: clearing out the underbrush', *Sociologica Ruralis*, XX(3), pp. 195–212.

Commission of European Communities, (1983), 'Le diagnostic énergétique: éléments de synthès, *Revue de l'Energie* No. 326, Paris, France.

Commission of European Communities (1984), *L'énergie et le développement. Quels enjeux? Quelles méthodes? Synthèses et conclusions*, Paris, Ed° Techniques et Documentation (Lavoisier), Paris, France.

Commission of European Communities (1985), *Drying of Food Products in the Developing Countries*, Directorate-General for Development, VIII/236/85, March.

Commission of European Communities, (1985), *Electric Power for Equipment in Remote Areas in the Developing Countries*, Directorate-General for Development, VIII/234/85, March.

Commission of European Communities, (1985), *Energy and Health Care in the Developing Countries*, Directorate-General for Development, VIII/233/85, March.

Commission of European Communities, (1985), *Renewable Sources of Energy and Village Water Supply in the Developing Countries*, Directorate-General for Development, VII/233/85, March.

Commission of European Communities, (1985), *Rural Electrification in the Developing Countries*, Directorate-General for Development, VIII/235/85, March.

Commission of European Communities, (1986), *Building the Renewable Energy Market in Developing Countries*, Directorate General for Development, VII/161/86-EN, February.

Commission of European Communities, (1986), 'Dossier: la crise du bois de feu' *Le Courrier*, No. 95, Brussels.

Commission of European Communities, (1987), *Energy Planning in the European Community and in the Third World*, Seminar at Luxembourg, 30 September to 3 October, 1986, Innotec Systemanalyse (ed.), Berlin.

Commission of European Communities, (1987), *Planning and Managing Energy in Rural Areas in Developing Countries: A Course Manual for a Two-week Training Programme*, Directorate General for Development.

Crawford, P.R. (1981), 'Implementation issues in Integrated Rural Development: a review of 21 USAID Projects', Integrated Rural Development Research Note 2, Development Alternatives Inc.

Crener, M., Leal, G., LeBlanc, R. and B. Thebaud, (1983), *Integrated Rural Development: state-of-the-art review*, Canadian International Development Agency, Quebec.

Cunty, G. (1979), 'Eoliennes et aérogénérateurs: Guide de l'énergie éolienne' EDISUD, Aix-en-Provence, France.

Daniel, P. (1985), 'A strategy for the rural poor in sub-Saharan Africa: towards oblivion or reconstruction', *Journal of Development Planning*, 15, pp. 113–136.

De Lepeleire G., K. Krishna Pasad, P. Verhaart, P. Visser, (1981), *Guide technique des fourneaux à bois*, EDISUD-BOIS DE FEU-ENDA-SKAT, Ed° Edisud, Aix-en-Provence, France.

de Montalembert, M.R. and J. Clement, (1983), *Fuelwood Supplies in the Developing Countries*, Forestry Paper No. 42, Food and Agricultural Organisation, Rome.

deLucia and Associates, (1986), 'Energy use in Pakistan's agricultural sector: an initial analysis and proposed TEM project', Report prepared for ENERCON, The National Energy Conservation Centre, Islamabad, Pakistan, November.

Desai, A.V. (1980), *India's Energy Economy: Facts and their Interpretation*, National Council of Applied Economic Research, New Delhi, India.

Desai, A.V. (1982), 'Technology transfer and development in the Indian tractor industry', mimeo, National Council of Applied Economic Research, New Delhi, India.

Devron, J.J., J. Egg & F. Lerin, (1979), *Biomasse: comparaison de valorisation des sous-produits agricoles*, GRET, Ministère de la Coopération, Paris, France.

Donald, G. (1976), *Credit for Small Farmers in Developing Countries*, Westview press, Boulder, Colorado.

Dorfman, R. and N.S. Dorfman, (eds) (1977), *Economics of the Environment*, W.W. Norton, New York.

Drabek, A.G. (ed.) (1987), 'Development alternatives: the challenge for NGOs', *World Development*, 15 (supplement), Autumn.

Dumon, R. (1982), *Valorisation énergétique du bois et de la biomasse*, Paris, Ed° Masson, Paris, France.

Eckholm, E.P. (1975), *The Other Energy Crisis: Fuelwood*, Worldwatch Paper No. 1, Worldwatch Institute, Washington, D.C.

EDF International, (no date), 'Electric power tariffing: example of tariffs construction based upon marginal costs', Paris, France.

Eicher, C.K. and D. Baker, (1982), 'Research on agricultural development in sub-Saharan Africa: A critical survey', Michigan State University Department of Agricultural Economics, *International Development Paper No. 1*, East Lansing, Michigan.

ENDA (1984), *Energie populaire dans le Tiers-Monde*, Dakar, Sénégal.

ESCAP and others, (1987), *Energy Manpower Analysis: A Manual for Planners*, Regional Energy Development Programme, ESCAP and ILO, April.

Falloux, F. and A. Mukendi, (1988), *Desertification Control and Renewable Resource Management in the Sahelian and Sudanian Zones of West Africa*, World Bank Technical Paper Number 70, Washington, D.C.

FAO (1975), *Organic material as fertiliser*, Report of a joint FAO/SIDA Expert Consultation, Rome, 1975.

FAO (1983), *The state of food and agriculture 1982*, Rome, 1983.

FAO (1983), *Woodfuel Surveys*, Forestry for local Community Development Programme, GCP/INT/365/SWE, Food and Agricultural Organisation, Rome, 1983.

FAO (1986), *Wood gas as an engine fuel*, FAO Forestry Paper 72, Rome, 1986.

FAO (1987), *Technical and Economic Aspects of Using Woodfuels in Rural Industries. Training in Planning National Programmes for Wood-based Energy*, FAO and Cooperazione Italiana Allo Sviluppo GCT/INT/433/ITA, October, p. 49.

Ferenczi, F. (1985), *Séchage des produits alimentaires dans les pays en développement*, CEC, Brussels.

Filloux, A. (1985), *Conversion thermique de l'énergie solaire. Fonctionnement et caractéristiques des capteurs solaires plans*, CSTB, Vaolbonne, France.

Fluitman, Fred, (1983), 'The socio-economic impact of rural electrification in developing countries: A review of experience', *World Employment Programme Research Working Paper*, WEP 2–22/WP 126, International Labour Organisation, November.

Foley, G. (1985), 'Woodfuel and conventional fuel demands in the developing world', *Ambio*, 14(4–5), Stockholm, Sweden.

Foley, G. (1987), 'Exaggerating the Sahelian woodfuel problem?', *Ambio*, 16(6), Stockholm, Sweden.

Foley, G. (1988a), 'Discussion paper on demand management', Paper presented to the World Bank Eastern and Southern Africa Regional Seminar on Household Energy Planning, Harare, Zimbabwe, 1–5 February 1988.

Foley, G. (1988b), 'The rural electrification dilemma', mimeo, The Panos Institute, 8 Alfred Place, London, March.

Foley, G. and G. Barnard, (1983), *Biomass Gasification in Developing Countries*, Technical Report 1, Energy Information Programme, Earth scan, London.

Foley, G. and P. Moss (1983), *Improved cooking stoves in developing countries*, Earthscan, International Institute for Environment and Development, London.

Geisler, G., B. Keller and P. Chuza, (1985), *The Needs of Rural Women in Northern Province*, Lusaka: National Commission for Development Planning.

GESTE (1988), *Autonomous Energy Production*, A Guide for Appropriate Industrial Technologies, Group for the Exchange of Science and Technology, Harmattan, Paris.

Gill, G.J. (1983b), 'Mechanised land preparation, productivity and employment in Bangladesh', *Journal of Developing Studies*, 19(3), April, 1983.

Gill, J. (1987), 'Improved Stoves in Developing Countries, A Critique', *Energy Policy*, Vol 15(2), 135-144 April.

Gill, J. (1983a), 'Fuelwood and stoves, lessons from Zimbabwe', in Prasad, K.K. and P. Verhaart (eds), *Wood Heat for Cooking*, Indian Academy of Sciences, Bangalore, India, 1983.

Gilmour, I., Harwood, C. and C. Kilroy, (1987), 'Wood and Woody Biomass use in agro-industries', a series of eight booklets on cocoa, coffee, tea and copra drying, prepared by the United Nations Pacific Energy Development Programme, Suva, Fiji.

Giri, J. (1983), *Le Sahel Demain – catastrophe ou renaissance?*, Ed° Karthala, Paris, France.

Giri, J. (1986), *L'Afrique en panne: vingt-cinq ans de développement*, Ed° Karthala, Paris, France.

Goupillon, J.F. (1983), 'Production d'énergie mécanique en petite et moyenne puissance par gazéfication de la biomass', avis et travaux du CEMAGREFF, Antony, France.

Grant, J.P. (1978), 'Disparity reduction rates in social indicators: a proposal for measuring the targeting progress in meeting basic needs', Overseas Development Council, Washington, D.C., Sept.

GRET (1980), *Biogaz: Eléments de bibliographie*, Ministère de la Coopération, Paris, France.

GRET-Collectif-F. Varagnat, (1984), *Document de travail Biogaz: Systèmes intégrés, Programmes de diffusion, Biogaz pour la motorisation*, AFME-GRET-GERES-Ministère de la Coopération, Paris, France.

GRET, (no date), *Lettre d'information documentaire*, 'Projet pilote sous-régional de l'information sur les énergies nouvelles et renouvelabes en Afrique de l'Ouest', Publication UNESCO réaliseée par le GRET, Paris, France.

GRET, Bruyère P., B. Gay, J. Sarda, (1984), *Les éoliennes de pompage*, GRET-IT DELLO, Gret, Paris, France.

GRET, Celaire R. (1987), *Les chaufe-eau solaires capteurs-stockeurs*, AFME-GRET-GERES-SYNOPSIS-Ministère de la Coopèration, Paris, France.

GRET, Maucor, J.B., S. Maucor (1984), *Micro-centrales hydrauliques* Ed° Alternatives, Paris, France.

GRET, Maucor J.P. (1980), *Les microcentrales hydrauliques* GRET-Ministère de la Coopération, Paris, France.

GRET-GERES (1983), *Les dossiers du biogaz* AFME-GRET-Ministère de la Coopération, Paris, France.

GRET-GERES (1984), *Biogaz* La Documentation Française, Paris, France.

GRET-GERES, (no date), *Le point sur le séchage*, Paris, France.

GRET-IT DELLO (no date), *Energies de pompage: approvisionnement en eau et énergie rurale* La Documentation Française, Paris, France.

Grut, M. (1986), 'Guidelines for identifying and preparing forestry projects', *Energy Department Paper No. 33*, World Bank, Washington, D.C.

Haentjens, A. & F. Maillard, (1985), *Energie et santé dans les pays en développement*, CEC, Brussels.

Hall, D., G. Barnard and P. Moss, (1982), *Biomass Energy in the Developing Countries: Current Role, Potential Problems and Prospects*, Pergamon Press Oxford.

157

Hardin, G. (1968), 'The tragedy of the commons', *Science*, 162, pp. 1243–1248, December 13.

Hathway, G. (1987), *Low Cost Vehicles: Options for Moving People and Goods*, Intermediate Technology Publications Ltd, London.

Hayami, Y. *et al*. (1979), *Agricultural Growth in Japan, Taiwan and the Philippines*, Asian Productivity Organisation, Tokyo.

Hill, R.N. (1980), 'A clamp can be appropriate for the burning of bricks', *Appropriate Technology*, 7(1), June.

Holdcroft, L.E. (1978), *The rise and fall of community development in developing countries, 1950–1960: A critical analysis and an annotated bibliography*, Michigan State University Department of Agricultural Economics, Rural Development Paper No. 2, East Lansing, Michigan.

Howes, M. (1982), *The potential for small-scale solar powered irrigation in Pakistan*, Institute of Development Studies, University of Sussex, UK.

Howes, M. (1985), *Rural Energy Surveys in the Third World*, Manuscript report IDRC-MR1907e, International Development Research Centre, Ottawa, May.

Hurst, C. (1983), 'Animal energetics: a proposed model of cattle and buffalo in the Indian sub-continent', *Biomass*, 3, pp. 135–149.

Hurst, C. (1983), 'Modelling energy use in agriculture: A case study in Bihar, India', *Working paper 190*, Institute of Development Studies, University of Sussex, November.

Hurst, C. (1984), 'A model of an Indian village: A study of alternative sources of energy for irrigation', *World Development*, 12(2), pp. 141–156, February.

Hurst, C. (1985), *Energy and Irrigation in India*, World Employment Programme, Working Paper 2–22/WP 154, International Labour Office, Geneva, September.

Hurst, C. (1986), 'Managing the commercialisation of solar energy technologies: A review of past experiences in developing countries, and an analysis of future policy implications', *World Employment Programme Working Paper*, WEP 2–22/WP 160, Feburary.

Hurst, C. (1988), 'Energy for small-scale engines', in A.V. Desai (ed.), *Energy Economics*, Wiley Eastern, New Delhi, India.

Hyman, E. (1986), 'The economics of improved charcoal stoves in Kenya', *Energy Policy*, 14.

IEPE (1989), *Energie internationale 88/89*, Ed° Economica, Paris, France.

IFRI (1989), 'Le monde et son évolution', *Rapport annuel RAMSES*, Ed° Dunod, Paris, France.

ILO (1975), 'Charcoal making for small-scale enterprises', International Labour Office, Geneva.

ILO (1983), *Training for Rural Electrification: a preliminary study*, International Labour Office, Geneva.

ILO (1984), *Small-scale Brickmaking*, International Labour Office, Geneva.

ILO (1986a), 'The rural energy crisis, women's work and basic needs', *Proceedings of an International Workshop*, The Hague, 21–24 April, International Labour Office, Geneva.

ILO (1986b), *Solar Drying: Practical Methods of Food Preservation*, International Labour Office, Geneva.

ILO (1987), *Linking energy with survival: A guide to energy, environment, and rural women's work*, International Labour Office, Geneva.

Institut Francophone de L'Energie, (1988), *Guide de L'Energie*, Ministere de la Cooperation et du Development, Paris.

Islam, M.N., Morse, R. and M.H. Soesastro, (1984), *Rural Energy to Meet Development Needs: Asian Village Approaches*, Westview, Boulder.

IT Power, (1985), *Wind Technology Assessment Study, Volume 1*, Reading, UK, February.

ITD (Institut Technologique DELLO) (1983), *L'eau en milieu rural dans les pays en développement*, Rapport de stage, Paris, France.

Jones, M. (1988), *Rural development: energy constraints, alternatives, and opportunties*, Institute for Energy Analysis, Oak Ridge Associated Universities, Washington, D.C., March.

Keddie, J. and W. Cleghorn, (1980), *Brick Manufacture in Developing Countries*, Scottish Academic Press, Edinburgh.

Khan, A.R. (1979), 'The Comilla model and the Integrated Rural Development Programme of Bangladesh: an experiment in co-operative capitalism', in *Agrarian Systems in Rural Development*, edited by Dharan Ghai, Azizur Rahman Khan, Eddy Lee, and Samir Padwan, Holmes and Meier, New York.

Kortem, D.C. (1980), 'Community organisation and rural development: a learning process', *The Public Administration Review*, 40(5), pp. 480-511.

Kuether, D.O. and J.B. Duff, (1981), 'Energy requirements of alternative rice production systems in the tropics', *IRRI Research Paper Series No. 59*, International Rice Research Institute, Phillipines.

Kumar, K. (1987), *A.I.D.'s Experience with Integrated Rural Development Projects*, A.I.D. Program Evaluation Report No. 19, Agency for International Development, Washington, D.C., July.

Lagandre, E. (1983), *Eléments pour penser le développement des énergies nouvelles et renouvelables dans le Tiers-Monde (des perspectives globales aux réalités de terrain)*, Publications DIRED, Paris, France.

Lagrange, B. (1979), *Biométhane*, 2 vol., Ed° EDISUD, Aix-en-Provence, France.

Lapillone, B. (1983), *L'approche MEDEES pour l'évaluation de la demande d'énergie dans les pays en développement*, IEPE, Grenoble, France.

Le Gourières, D. (1980), *Energie éolienne: théorie, conception et calcul pratique des installations*, Ed° Eyrolles, Paris, France.

Leach, G. (1986), *Energie et coirssance*, Butterworths, UK.

Leach, G. and M. Gowan, (1987), *Household Energy Handbook: An Interim Guide and Reference Manual*, World Bank Technical Paper Number 67, Washington, D.C.

Leach, G. and R. Mearns, (1988), *Bioenergy Issues and Options for Africa*, International Institute for Energy and Development, London.

Leach, G. (1987), *Household Energy in South Asia*, Elsevier Applied Science, London.

Lenoir, R. (1984), *Le Tiers Monde peut se nourrir*, Ed° Fayard, Paris, France.

Lichtman, R. (1987), 'Organisational manpower and institutional aspects of biogas in India', in Bhatia, R. and A.F. Peirera (eds), *Socioeconomic Aspects of Renewable Energy Technologies*, International Labour Office, Geneva.

Lipton, M. (1977), *Why Poor People Stay Poor: Urban Biases in World Development*, Temple Smith, London.

Lipton, M. (1981), 'Agricultural finance and rural credit in poor countries', in P. Streeton and R. Jolly (eds), *Recent Issues in World Development*, Pergamon Press, Oxford.

Lipton, M. (1987), 'Limits of price policy for agriculture: which way for the World Bank?', *Development Policy Review*, 5(2), pp. 197–215, June.

Lipton, M. (1968), 'The theory of the optimising peasant', *Journal of Development Studies*, XIV(1).

Little, E.C.S. (1975), 'A kiln for charcoal making in the field', *Tropical Science*, XIV(3).

McCall, M. (1984), *Persuading People to Use Appropriate Technology: an account of an RET Project in Tanzania*, Technology and Development Group, Twente University of Technology, Enschede, the Netherlands.

Mackie, C. (1986), *Forestry in Asia: USAID's experience*, Division of Natural Resources, Office of Technical Resources, Bureau for Asia and the Near East, USAID, Washington, D.C. 20523, November.

Madon, G. & N. Matly, (1986), *Le secteur bois-énergie au Sahel: élements pour une stratégie d'intervention*, New York, UNSO.

Maillard, F. & Vernet, (1985), *Electrification rurale dans les pays en développement*, CEC, Brussels.

Makhijani, (1975), *Energie et agriculture dans le Tiers-Monde*, Ballinger Publishing Company, USA.

Makhijani, A. and A. Poole, (1975), *Energy and Agriculture in the Third World*, Ballinger, Cambridge, Mass.

Manibog, F. (1984), 'Improved cooking stoves in the developing countries: problems and opportunities', *Annual Review of Energy*, 9, p 199–227.

Mayer, A. *et al* (1958), *Pilot Project, India*, University of California Press, Berkely.

Meunier, B. (1983), *Electrification des atolls en Polynésie: comparaison entre diesel et générateur photovoltaïque* AFME, Paris, France.

Michaïlof, S. (1987), *Les apprentis sorciers du développement: Mythes technocratiques face à la pauvreté rurale*, Ed° Economica, Paris, France.

Ministère de la Coopération det du Développement (1988), *Guide de l'énergie*, éd SEPIA, Paris, France.

Molle, J.F. (1982), *Energie d'origine agricole. Les filières thermochimiques de valorisation de la biomasse*, CEMA-GREFF, Antony, France.

Moniton, L., M. Le Nir, J. Roux (1981), *Les micro-centrales hydroélectriques*, Ed° Masson, Paris, France.

Moris, Jon, (1981), *Managing Induced Rural Development*, International Development Institute, Bloomington, Indiana.

Munasinghe, M. (1987), *Rural Electrification for Development: Policy Analysis and Applications*, Westview Special Studies in Natural Resources and Energy Management, Boulder, Colorado.

Newcombe, K. (1984), 'An economic justification for rural afforestation: The case of Ethiopia', *Energy Department Paper No. 16*, World Bank, Washington, D.C.

Nolle, J. (no date), *Machines modernes à traction animale: itinéraire d'un inventeur au service des petits paysans*, L'Harmattan, Paris, France.

Novak, M. (1988), 'Le Grameen Bank au Bangladesh', *Histoires de developpement No, 1*, Cahiers de l'institut social de Lyon, France, 1988.

Nowak, M. & J.C. Devèze, (1987), *Compte rendu de mission auprès de la Grameen Bank au Bangladesh*, CCCE, Paris, France.

Office of Energy, (1986), *Small Power Systems for Economic Development in Rural Areas*, Agency for International Development, Washington, D.C., October.

Patel, S.M. and R.K. Gupta, (1979), *Study on Conservation of Light Diesel Oil Used in Pumpsets for the Irrigation in Gujarat State*, Institute of Cooperative Management, Ellisbridge, Ahmedabad, India, January.

PEDP, (1986), *A summary of energy use statistics obtained from household energy surveys in Pacific Island Countries*, United Nations Pacific Energy Development Programme Report REG 86.3, Suva, Fiji.

Percebois, J. (1989), 'Les prix de l'énergie dans les pays en développement', *Revue de l'Energie*, No. 407, Paris, France.

Pereira, A.F. and R. Bhatia (eds), *Renewable Energy Technologies for Rural Development: Lessons from Country Experiences*, International Labour Office, Geneva, forthcoming.

Pereira, A.F. (1985), 'Constraints to the diffusion of small-scale solar driers and policy implications', in *Energy Conserving Technologies for the Post-Harvest System*, Agricultural Centre, Przysiek, Poland, in collaboration with the United Nations University.

Prior, M. (1984), 'Fuel use in urban areas in Bangladesh', Working Paper No. 40, Bangladesh Energy Planning Project, Planning Commission, Dhaka, Bangladesh.

Raskin, P.D. (1986), *LEAP: A Description of the LDC Energy Alternatives Planning Model*, Energy Environment and Development in Africa, No. 8, Beijer Institute/Scandinavian Institute of African Stujdies, Sweden.

Reddy, A.K.N. (1985), 'The energy and economic implications of agricultural technologies: An approach based on the technical options for the operations of crop production', *World Employment Programme Working Paper*, WEP 2–22/WP 149, International Labour Office, Geneva, June.

Repetto, R. and T. Holmes, (1983), 'The role of population in resource depletion in developing countries', *Population and Development Review*, 9(4), pp. 609–632, December.

Riviére, M. (1987), *Valorisation de la biomase des cannes à sucre à l'île de la Rénion* Les dossiers de l'outre-mer No. 86, Bulletin d'information du CENADDOM, Talence.

Rocher, P. (1985), *Les énergies renouvelables dans les départements et territoires d'outre-mer*, Diaporama AFME, Paris, France.

Rondinelli, D.A. and K. Ruddle, (1978), 'Coping with poverty in international development policy: An evaluation of spatially integrated development', *World Development*, 6(4), pp. 479–347.

Ruttan, V.W. (1984), 'Integrated rural development programmes: a historical perspective', *World Development*, 12(94), pp. 393–401.

Sanghi, A. and M.G. Blase, (1976), 'An economic analysis of energy requirements of alternative farming systems for small farmers: some policy issues', *Indian Journal of Agricultural Economics*, pp. 179–191, July–September.

Santerre, M.T. and K.R. Smith (1982), 'Measures of appropriateness: the resource requirement of anaerobic digestion (biogas) systems', *World Development*, 10(3), pp. 239-261.

Saunders, R.J. and J.J. Warford, (1976), *Village Water Supply: Economics and Policy in the Developing World*, The Johns Hopkins University Press for the World Bank, Baltimore.

Scandizzo, P.L. and J.L. Dillon, (1979), 'Peasant agriculture and risk preferences in Northeast Brazil: a statistical sampling approach', in J.A. Roumasset (ed.), *Risk, Uncertainty and Agricultural Development*, Agricultural Development Council, New York.

SEED-M Matly, (no date), *Biomasse – Energie et développement, une stratégie possible en développement*, La Documentation Française, Paris, France.

SEMA, (1981), *Evaluation des énergies renouvelables pour les pays en développement*, Collection Technologies et Développement, Ed° Min. de la Coopération-COMES (AFME), Paris, France.

SEMA, (1985), *Stratégie française de coopération dans le domaine de la biomasse*, Ministère de la Coopération-AFME, Paris, France.

Shanahan, Y. (1986), 'Woodfuel and the rural household', *The Courier*, ACP-European Community, 95, January–February.

Sharma, S.N. (1988), *Institutional and Organisational Aspects of Promoting the Use of Water Turbines in Nepal*, World Employment Programme Working Paper (WEP 2–22/WP 181), International Labour Office, Geneva.

SIDA, (1984), *Solar Water Heating in Developing Countries*, Swedish International Development Agency, Industry Division, S-105 25, Stockholm, Sweden, March.

162

Smith, K., Aggarwal, A.L. and R.M. Dave, (1983), 'Air pollution and rural biomass fuels in developing countries: A pilot study in India and implications for research and policy', *Atmospheric Environment*, 17(11), pp. 2343–2362.

Spears, J. (1986), 'Deforestation, fuelwood consumption, and forest conservation: an action program for FY86–88', mimeo, World Bank, Washington, D.C.

Starr, M.R. and W. Paltz, (1983), *Photovoltaic Power for Europe: An Assessment Study*, Solar Energy R and D in the European Community, Series C, Volume 2.

Stout, B.A. (1979), *Energy for World-Wide Agriculture*, Agriculture Series No. 7, FAO, Rome.

Streeten, P.D. and S.J. Burki, (1979), 'Basic needs: some issues', *World Development*, 6(3), pp. 411–421.

Streeten, P.D. (1987), *What Price Food?*, Macmillan, London.

Stuckey, D.C. (1983), *Biogas in Developing Countries: A Critical Appraisal*, paper presented at the 3rd International Symposium on Anaerobic Digestion, Boston, U.S.A., August.

Systèmes Solaires (Revue) (1985), Numéro spécial Tiers-Monde, Paris, France.

Systèmes Solaires, Numéro spécial (1986), 'Panorama mondial de l'énergie éolienne', Paris, France.

Taylor, R.P. (1983), *Decentralised Renewable Energy Technology Development in China*, World Bank Staff Working Paper 535, World Bank, Washington, D.C.

Tendller, J, (1979), *Rural Electrification: Linkages and Justifications*, AID Program Evaluation Discussion Paper No. 3, USAID, April.

Thery, D., M. Nacro, E. Lagrande (1983), 'Pratique du biogaz le Tiers-Monde, Chinese Sud, Haute Volta, Sénégal', doc. 17, ENDA, Dakar-Sénégal.

Tropical Products Institute, (1980), 'Charcoal production using a transportable metal kiln', *Rural Technology Guide 12*, London.

United Nations-AFME (1986), 'Séminaire sur la viabilité technico-économique des petits systèmes utilisant les énergies renouvelables dans les pays en développement', Document de base, Sophia Antipolis, France.

USAID, (1984), 'Short and long term impact of USAID/Haiti's agroforestry outreach project limited by lower than average tree survival and growth rates and deficient research techniques', *Audit report number 1–521–84–8*, US Agency for International Development, Washington, D.C.

USAID, (1985), *Private Enterprise Development*, A.I.D. Policy Paper, Agency for International Development, Washington, D.C.

Vaing, C. (1986), *Deux filières compétives de valorisation énergétique de la biomasse par le procédé de la gazéification thermochimique*, CEEMAT, Antony, France.

Vauge, C. (1981), *Lexique des énergies renouvelables*, Ed° SCM, Paris, France.

Visser, P. and P. Verhaart, (1980), 'Experiments with the open fire', in K.K. Prasad (ed), *Some Performance Tests on Open Fires and the Family Cooker*,

Woodburning Stove Group, Technical University of Eindhoven, Eindhoven, The Netherlands.

VITA, (1980), *Making charcoal*, Volunteers in Technical Assistance, Washington, D.C.

Von Pischke, J.D. *et al.* (eds) (1983), *Rural Financial Markets in Developing Countries: Their Use and Abuse*, Johns Hopkins University Press, Baltimore.

Wade, R. (1987), 'The management of common property resources: Finding a cooperative solution', *The World Bank Research Observer*, 2(2), pp. 2190–234, July.

Ward, G.M., Sutherland, T.M. and J.M. Sutherland, (1980), 'Animals as an energy source in Third World agriculture', *Science*, 208(9).

Ward, M., Ashworth, J.H. and G. Burril, (1984), *Renewable Energy Technologies in Africa: An Assessment of Field Experience and Future Directions*, U.S. Agency for International Development, Washington, D.C. April.

Wolgin, J.M. (1975), 'Resource allocation and risk: a case study of smallholder agriculture in Kenya', *American Journal of Agricultural Economics*.

World Bank, (1975), *Rural electrification*, Washington, D.C.

World Bank, (1976), *Electrification rurale*, Washington.

World Bank, (1978), *Forestry: Sector policy paper*, Washington, D.C.

World Bank, (1979), 'Behaviour of foodgrain production and consumption in India, 1960–77', *World Bank Staff Working Paper 339*, Washington, D.C.

World Bank, (1983), *Energy and Transport in Developing Countries: Towards Achieving Greater Energy Efficiency*, Transport and Water Department, World Bank, Washington, D.C. February.

World Bank, (1985a), *Desertification in the Sahelian and Sudanian zones of West Africa*, Washington, D.C.

World Bank, (1985b), 'Test results on kerosene and other stoves for developing countries', *Energy Department Paper No. 27*, World Bank, Washington, D.C.

World Bank, (1986), *Test results on charcoal stoves from developing countries*, Joint UNDP/ World Bank Energy Sector Management Assistance Program, World Bank, Washington, D.C., December.

World Bank, (1986), *World Development Report 1986*, Washington, D.C.

World Bank, (1987), 'Rapport sur le développement dans le Monde', *Rapport 1987*, Washington, D.C.

World Bank (1987a), 'Review of household energy issues in Africa', Draft working paper, Energy Policy and Advisory Division, Energy Department, World Bank, Washington, D.C., May.

World Bank, (1987c), *Community Water Supply: The Handpump Option*, A joint contribution by the United Nations Development Programme and the World Bank to the International Drinking Water Supply and Sanitation Decade, Washington, D.C.

World Bank, (1988), *Some Considerations in Collecting Data on Household Energy Consumption*, Industry and Energy Department Working Paper No, 3, World Bank, Washington, D.C., March.

164

World Bank, (1989), *World Development Report*, Washington, D.C.

World Bank/Halcrow, (1983), *Small-scale Solar-Powered Pumping Systems: The Technology, its Economics and its Advancement*, World Bank, Washington, D.C.

Annex IV: List of experts consulted during the production of the guide[1]

Dr Youba Sokona,
ENDA-TM,
BP 3370,
Dakar,
Senegal.

Dr Armand Pereira,
ILO,
CP 500,
CH 1211,
Geneva,
Switzerland.

Gustavo Best,
Energy and Environment Group,
FAO,
Via delle Terme di Caracalla,
00100 Roma,
Italy.

Gerald Leach,
IIED,
3 Endsleigh Street,
London WCD1H 0DD.
UK.

Dr Wim Hulsher,
Technology and Development
Group,
Twente University,
PO Box 217,
7500 AE Enschede,
The Netherlands.

Professor Ramesh Bhatia,
Institute of Economic Growth,
University of Delhi,
Delhi 110007,
India.

Dr Amara Pongsapich,
Social Research Institute,
CUSRI,
Chulalongkorn University,
Phay Thai Road,
Bangkok 10500,
Thailand.

Mr P.J. Johnston,
Pacific Energy Development
Programme,
c/o UNDP,
Private Bag,
Suva,
Fiji.

Dr Herbert Wade,
PEDP,
Institute des Energies
Renouvelables (IERPS),
BP11530,
Mahina,
Polynesie Francaise.

Haile Lul Tebike,
Energy Advisor to the ECA,
PO Box 3005,
Addis Ababa,
Ethiopia.

1. While every effort was taken to incorporate the comments of the expert reviewers, this was not possible in all cases (for instance where experts had conflicting opinions) and they are not responsible for any errors or omissions that remain.